It's Jacob!

My Name Is Jacob!
What's Yours?

By

Jacob Bergen

ISBN: 0-7596-9535-0 (softcover)
ISBN: 0-7596-9534-2 (ebook)

This book is printed on acid free paper.

1stBooks - rev. 3/22/02

I would like to dedicate this book to my wife for all the encouragement I received from her during the process. I have bounced ideas off her many times. Sometimes I pushed her ideas aside at first; then after some reflection I often took her advice.

I also want to thank a friend of mine, Danny Chau: Who also challenged my ideas on cover design, and other things. Without his input I would have made some wrong turns in these areas. Thanks Dan.

Thanks Celeste for calling me Jacob, it was instrumental in the selection of the Title.

I also want to dedicate this book to my sister Helen who just went to be with Jesus, November 25/ 1998, 10:30 A.M., and Fred her husband. One day Helen saw Chapter Four: Presenting The Ladies, and made a remark about how I presented it. It was one of those jokingly snide remarks.

Helen and Fred, and my wife and I were very close friends, as well as being family. We shared little quirks, which we loaded up on each other from time to time; especially, things to do with men versus women; in the light of the Bible.

Fred and I usually referred to ourselves as men who were no wimps. Every so often we did something that might put us in the category of being a wimp. One such time was when the ladies made us a T- Shirt with our children's picture on it. After we were conned into wearing it we were jokingly thought of as: You guessed it, Wimps.

Just because The Lord is now being mentioned as the last one to whom I dedicate this book, does not make him least in importance; It does in fact make him first. The Bible says that the last shall be first. The Bible also says of him: He is the Alfa and Omega: The First and The Last.

It is because of him and through my Lord that I was in all ways capable of writing this book.

Thanks be to God!

Jacob Bergen

Preface

Jacob, the patriarch, is a subject that can lead to the writing of a volume of books. The interest in this character of the Bible is probably not as great on the level of the average person, as it is with scholars, Bible teachers, ministers, etc. The usual matter of interest that Jacob generates is, how he fits in with the nation of Israel. When the aforementioned people think about writing about Jacob, for the most part their considerations are historical. Jacob is probably covered in detail in the Bible schools around the world, in the historical sense. The next most prominent feature of this man is that he was a deceiver.

Jacob was much more than just historical, and a deceiver. I firmly believe that Jacob was a man that was a very deep thinker. I believe that he was a man who had a heart for people. This seems to be a contradiction in terms when one considers how selfish he was in the early part of his life. I believe that Jacob loved very deeply. I know that Jacob loved deeply on the physical plain, and I have become convinced that he loved in depth on the spiritual level as well.

Jacob is a man of many faces. He is intricate and confusing. Jacob is also so predictable that you could almost predict his every mood, and move. When you begin to know the man, he becomes a personality with whom we can relate. Jacob's life is an open book, for all who have the time to read the pages of his life. Jacob is a man who presents me with a volume as colorful as the color scale itself. If I were an artist, I could paint a canvas that would take a mass of space to fill in the details.

I have come to the conclusion that Jacob is: Jacob Bergen, Billy Graham, Abraham Lincoln, Florence Nightingale, Sarah, Abraham, and Adam, etc. I am sure that within the walls of every human being there is a swatch of Jacob. Beating within the heart of every person there is a heart like that of Jacob. I believe that everyone has at one time or another been tempted to one degree or another, to be deceptive.

The deception that some folks portray is almost considered cute, because it is so minuscule. In others the deception they exhibit, is on such a grand scale that it is impossible to miss seeing it as being The Big Scam of all time.

It does not matter to what degree deception is used; it remains under the same heading,

Falsehood.

When I look in the thesaurus, I am confronted with a list of definitions that includes words like: concealment, fakery, illusion, ploy, joke, pretense, bluff or trick…Some of these words are not very intimidating when I put them on a scale of 1-10. Some of them are humorous, but they are still related to the root word.

Deception.

When I think of Jacob, this flaw of deception has always been the first thing that I have thought of about the man. I wonder, what is the first thing that you think about when you see me, or hear someone talk about me. Then when I see you, or hear someone talk about you, what is the first thing that I think about you?

Even though Jacob was a cheat, I wonder if it was the trait, which caused the greatest impact on other people. I believe that some of the other intense character traits that he displayed are far more important than his attributes of deceit. Jacob was a man who loved, with a passion so great, that he played favoritism. Who among us has not been guilty?

Three of the people that Jacob loved most were: Rachel, Joseph, and Benjamin. He showed favoritism in every case. I love my wife, and I will favor her above all others. There can be right, and there can be wrong in favoring one person over another.

Favoritism is so real in society that it could be defined to make it look as though it should be a rite. Does this change the meaning of it? Two of the words related to favoritism are: Injustice, and one-sidedness. How does that sound to you, in the light of your treatment of others?

There are extremes, and there are moderate infractions in this arena. Have all of us not suffered from these ills at one time or another? I think that all it takes for us to analyze this, is that we take a serious look at the life that we live, and in all honesty, admit to the areas that the glove fits our hand.

Everything, which I have reflected on, is real life. Everything, that is past, is unchangeable. Nevertheless, if we are bold enough to realize that we have participated in matters of adversity, which have caused hurts in the past; can we not try to do something about those matters in the future?

In the manuscript you have before you, I will have endeavored to explain the life of Jacob, in ways that are colorful. At times my descriptive terms fall into the path of a hypothesis. Hypothetical references are those that are not factual.

As you read this book: It's Jacob! My Name Is Jacob! What's Yours?

Read it and weep.
Read it and laugh.
Read it and learn.
Read it and love.

Read it, and fall in love with Him: who is able to keep you from falling, and is able to preserve you until that day when you meet Him face to face.

Read it to love Jesus more.

Jacob Bergen

Finally my brethren, be strong in the Lord, and in the power of his might. Put on the whole armor of God, that ye may be able to stand against the wiles of the devil. For we wrestle not against flesh and blood, but against principalities, against powers, against the rulers of the darkness of this world, against spiritual wickedness in high places.

Wherefore, take unto you the whole armor of God, that ye may be able to withstand in the evil day, and having done all, to stand. Stand therefore, having your loins girt about with truth, and having on the breastplate of righteousness; And your feet shod with the preparation of the gospel of peace; Above all, taking the shield of faith, wherewith ye shall be able to quench all the fiery darts of the wicked.

And take the helmet of salvation, and the sword of the Spirit, which is the word of God: Praying always with all prayer and supplication in the Spirit, and watching thereunto with all perseverance and supplication for all saints; Ephesians 6:10-18

My help comes from my Lord, Who made everything.

Contents

◈

◈

Part One
People From My Past

◈

◈

◈

Part Two
Who Gets The Family Farm

◈

◈

◈

Part Three
Jacob The Puzzle

◇
◇
◇

Part Four
Till Death Do Us Part

◇
◇
◇

Part Five
A Couple of Short Stories

Introduction

The title I have chosen should say a great deal about the book you are contemplating reading. At first glance, you might think that it is a story about me: The author. Actually, this is far from the truth of the matter.

Although I relate to some segments of my life throughout the book, I am engrossed in something that is more far reaching than what people know about me, Jacob Bergen. When you look at the title, I hope that the first thing that you will wonder about is: "Whom is he talking about?"

The next thing that I hope for is that something on the cover will tell you the answer to that question. I hope that you will be prompted to realize that there are at least three persons, and a presence, represented on the cover display.

Thirdly, I hope that you will recognize that one of the persons who is more present than anyone else, either in pictorial form, or in the unseen portion of the cover, is more important than all the rest.

I could go name by name and give you a list of answers, but I won't. Your homework, should you accept the challenge, is this: Look for the answers. If you find the answers on your own, I believe that you will end up the better person for it by the time you reach the end of this book.

Thanks for taking the time to read this manuscript.

Part One

People From My Past

Jacob Bergen

Roots

The art of deception is part of the nature of people. The Bible speaks of the heart of people being deceitful, and desperately wicked. This statement leaves one with the realization that it is an extreme situation. The verse goes on to say: "Who can know it?"

With this thought in mind, we need to remember that we are no exception to the rule. We do not want to give the impression that we are so much better, simply because we do not do this, that or the other. Just remember that God can and does use all kinds of people to fulfill his purposes.

Jacob Bergen

Chapter 1

I named this book in the fashion I did, for a specific reason. It was not because my name is Jacob. Just because my name is Jacob is no reason to write a book. Everybody here has a wonderful name; I am sure of that. Your name may be Tom, Ruth, or Jim, which in is no reason to write on the subject. I feel that we need to have a more solid basis than just someone's name, to do a manuscript.

If I selected the name Tom, and put it into the book title that read: My Name Is Tom, I would want it to represent something relevant enough for people to have an interest in it. If this title represented a person like Tom Landry, then most people would know what this book might relate to. Those, who do not know of Tom, will find out that football is his forte.

When I think of the name Ruth, I think of the current crop of choices first. In so doing I reflect on Ruth Graham. She is the wife of Billy Graham. When I think of people in the past I think of Ruth in the Bible. While thinking of her, my mind goes into the mode of a love story. The story of Ruth and Naomi is a fantastic picture of love: Not easily paralleled by any other love story. I consider the story of: "For God so loved the world,..." Jn. 3:16 far greater.

When I am browsing through the Christian bookstore I see books about people like Tom Landry, and Ruth Graham. This gives me a reason to explore avenues of interest in their lives. Tom Landry's name registers in my mind when I think of football coaches. Another thing that I reflect upon when I think of him is that he is also a Christian professional. Now we are in a realm where any one of us could be interested in a book about him. The reason for our interest may be because he is trying to show his Christianity at work in real life.

When I think of the name Ruth in this setting, I can also relate to something of interest. I might be interested in knowing what the wife of a man such as Billy Graham might have to offer the Christian reader. Maybe, I would just want to find out if I had missed something important in the book of Ruth.

Well, what about Jim? Good question: No answer. When I think about Jim, I think of food. Jim and Eileen do most of the banquets in our church: No offense Jim. Now, this is what I relate to when I think of Jim.

Now, if someone wrote a book, and titled it: My name is Jim, many folks may run out and buy a dozen copies to pass out to their friends. It may be a great book on how to do banquets, and that is great. Nevertheless, we do not all do banquets.

Let's move onto my next searching thought. When this book graces the shelf of the local bookstore, will it send chills of excitement through your anatomy? I hope so. Possibly, if the title gets your attention, the introduction overwhelms your mind, and your browser scans a few pages; finally, the interest level may have peaked: You buy the book. That is good for me, and prayerfully it will be beneficial to your spiritual health.

It was my full intention to lure suspecting souls to the cover of this book, when I chose the name. It was not my intention though, to bring it to your attention: Just to make your acquaintance with the author. That is an incidental matter. My intent goes far deeper than that. Many people would immediately relate to a time of old testament history, if they heard the words: My Name Is Jacob!

My purpose is to display the life of a man whom they called a scoundrel. This was done with many different words. Over the centuries, Jacob's name has been torn apart because of what he was. The Bible plainly leaves us with the impression that he was a cheat.

Before we can take a good look at which rung of the ladder Jacob aspired to, we are going to have to explore where he came from. This will entail exploration of his roots.

Many people may remember a book entitled "Roots," it was written by Alex Halley. It was the account of many struggles that the Negro people faced. As I watched it in the movie version, I found myself bathed in compassion; as they showed the trials of life faced by these people. Alex Halley went back to before his time to get the facts. This is what I need to do.

Simple historical fact does not usually thrill too many people. For instance, many readers may not care much when or where I was born. The color of my skin or the level of bills in my bank account may not necessarily be important to most people.

It has been very hard for me to start writing this book while I have been considering the life of Jacob; though the subject matter Jacob has always been a point of interest to me personally.

Maybe this is my position because Jacob and I share first names. Names that make people think of someone, as a cheater are not really that endearing. If I go back and find out the reasons behind his descriptive nametag, his story (history) becomes a bit more alluring to me.

From the time that I was just a boy, I was called Jakey. People always want to add something to our name. Instead of calling me Jake or Jacob, they felt they liked Jakey. It reminds me of the world in which we are living. People call someone Mikey, instead of Mike. Or they will call someone like Mike Vernon (a hockey goaltender) Vernie.

After awhile, they just called me Jake. Finally, people just started calling me Jack. Jack does not mean Jacob at all. As time went on I went by the name of Jack. It was easier than always trying to say: *My Name Is Jacob!*

Recently I heard a preacher say: "If your name is Jacob, be proud of it." I finally felt like shouting: My Name is Jacob! When he pointed out what Jacob became, rather than what he started as, I got excited. Eventually, during a name change, God called Jacob: "...A Prince with God."

Look at it. We seem to have a monumental character change. One day he is a cheater, the next day he is wearing Princely robes. If I were just to say that Jacob became a Prince with God, then we may not get to know anything else about the man. Nothing, about how the details in the life of this man can help us through the same kind of struggles, may ever become apparent.

This story is not only about a man called Jacob. It is about all of us. It is about everyday life. To be specific, this is why each of us should get excited about the history of a man like this. Each of us in this world has a wealth of insight and experience, to offer the world around us. Our individual heritage is worth vast amounts of gold, if calculated for value sake alone.

Any one of us may say: "My heritage is not worth a dime. 'I came from a family of losers.' 'I never had a real chance in life.' " Your thoughts may be well founded. However, if we have come to realize this, then we are in the position of being able to do something about it.

When we come to realize that there has been a wrong perpetration of the day's offerings, it's our move: Somehow, we should be able to make things right.

If I put the whole story of Jacob on a spreadsheet, I would have to include many details. Parents, grandparents, and even great grandparents, would be important, to bring a proper balance to what the life of Jacob was all about. My intention is to take us from the very possibility that he would be born, to the reality of the impact that he had on the human race.

When the Jews refer to God, they refer to the God of Abraham, Isaac, and Jacob. We have a continuum here that begins at Abraham. What about Abraham? The story of Abraham really began with Noah. The reason I say the story of Abraham really begins with Noah is that this was a beginning. We literally have to go back to Adam to get the whole picture.

Remember, Noah was a man who walked with God: This is imperative. When the flood ended, and his family was left to populate the earth, they began by having a Godly legacy. The Bible says that Noah "Walked with God."

Somewhere along the way, something began to fall apart: Concerning the family walking with God. Instead of checking with God as to their future, they set out to plan it for themselves. People began to believe that they needed to make a name for themselves. As a result of this, they set out to build a city, one with a high tower. Our High Tower is God. Nevertheless, it was not the intent of these people to make this God their great support. Hence: The Tower of Babel.

God really did not appreciate the results of their planning sessions, so he changed their plans for them. He scattered them around the country, and gave them all different languages. In time, Abraham's direct descendants found themselves at a place called Ur of the Chaldees.

Ur became a booming metropolis. It was a place infested with idol worshipers. Nanna was the moon God. They worshiped it here at Ur. History evidences the fact that Nanna was found in people's homes. Abraham grew up in this kind of idol worshiping culture.

Along with the worship habits being against God's law, they must have taken on other bad habits. In business, if we are not on course with God's ways, unscrupulous dealings are the result.

Abraham's great-grandfather, and his grandfather deeply entrenched in this idol worshiping culture. Nevertheless, a transition took place when God came and made it clear to Abraham that he was to leave this setting: To go elsewhere.

In Genesis 11, we will see that Terah (Abraham's father), Abraham, and his wife Sarah, and Terah's grandson Lot, left the city of Ur. As I look backward from Abraham to Noah, I see a very good trait beginning to take shape in Abraham. God told Noah that he would destroy all flesh because of sin. He also told him to build an ark for the safety of his family.

He built the ark, so he must have believed the word of God. Faith is the tremendous trait I see transferred from Noah to Abraham. The road between the two is not one built on a legacy of faith. Nevertheless, Abraham believed God during this time.

Extreme faith is evident in this man: Whom they called a friend of God. At this juncture we become aware of a major promise. We often hear of the promise of God. Listen to one of the promises with me: " I will make of thee a great nation, and I will bless thee, and make thy name great, and thou shalt be a blessing: And I will bless them that bless thee, and curse him that curseth thee; and in thee shall all the families of the earth be blessed."

Genesis 12:2-3

Another transition that takes place as we move along is in Genesis 12:18 "And in thy seed shall all the nations of the earth be blessed, because thou hast obeyed my voice." I can see a transfer of power and responsibility from one generation to another taking place here.

Now, just because Abraham is called a friend of God, does not mean that he was perfect. Times were, when God said go this way, Abraham went the other. However, if we look at the overall picture, he was obedient to the call of God. When Abraham first left Ur of the Chaldees, he went without knowing exactly where God wanted him to go. He was left with a promise, and he accepted that as enough to obey the command.

The place he went to at the beginning was a place called Haran. Haran, means roads. This is the place where Abraham lived till he had direction from the Lord. It was a good place for that; because it was a crossroads from which he could go in many directions. Haran was to be an important reference point in the life of his son, and his grandson (Jacob).

The seemingly inbred faith of Abraham definitely had its share of tumult. At the age of 100 he still did not have a son. If he were to be the

9

father of many nations, as promised by God, Abraham was going to need to raise a family.

Finally, in line with the promise of God, a son was born. Many instances in this account could use a better explanation, but it would almost require another work on its own to do it justice.

One of the greatest tests of his love for God came at the expense nearly losing the son. Nevertheless, the character of this man was such that it was God first, whether he understood what was going on or not. I am beginning to see that he has much to pass on to his children. Abraham became a very wealthy man, and we will see that this part of his heritage carried on through his son, and grandson Jacob.

Abraham lived to be 175 years old. I mentioned that we would go from the very possibility of Jacob's birth, to his overall impact on the human race. This began when God spoke in Genesis 22:18: "And in thy seed shall all the nations of the earth be blessed."

The word seed takes us one step closer to Jacob. I have begun to set out a bit of a reference bank with which to compare Jacob with his roots. One thing that Jacob was known for was that of being a deceiver. Abraham has not yet shown us that he had deception in his blood. It will become evident that he also had a bit of a problem with deception. Just so we can draw a parallel, I will portray it now.

When Abraham went to Egypt, he had to cover his tracks. He seemed to finish the run in fear of the Pharaoh. He told Pharaoh that his wife was his sister. Because his wife was a good looker, Abraham thought deception would be the answer to his problem. He thought Pharaoh would take his wife, and maybe his life. Pharaoh found out and sent the whole clan packing.

When we read the passage of scripture in Genesis 12, Egypt was evidently not the brightest spot of his trip. Most of what we see in Abraham was good, but his flaw was the same as ours: He was born into the human race. Nevertheless, God carried him through.

As we persist, we can see how this pattern was to repeat itself. The faithfulness of God will be evident throughout the book. God was faithful to the patriarchs, and he will be faithful to us.

I have drawn just a small picture of the life of Jacob. I am looking forward to meeting Jacob's dad Isaac. He was a wonderful man. As we put the pieces together, I am sure we will see why Jacob was the way he was in his early years: And what he was in the outcome.

Preparing for Jacob

And Isaac entreated the LORD for his wife, because she was barren: and the LORD was entreated of him, and Rebekah his wife conceived. And the children struggled together within her; and she said, if it be so, why am I thus? And she went to enquire of the LORD. And the LORD said unto her, two nations are in thy womb, and two manner of people shall be separated from thy bowels; and the one people shall be stronger than the other people; and the elder shall serve the younger. Genesis 25: 21-28

Chapter 2

In my preparation to bring Jacob onto the scene, I find that I am still hanging onto Abraham. The contents of his life are so vast that they occupy unlimited space. When it came time to expect God to begin to fulfill the promise to give Abraham and Sarah a son, life around the farm got interesting. Finally, God said a son would enter his home: It was a shocker. Abraham had a difficult time adjusting to this enlightenment.

Sometimes we think God is kidding when speaks to us. It may appear as though God is telling a joke. I do not intend any disrespect in making this statement. Some men and women in the Bible questioned the word of God.

According to my research, notable men and women in the Bible were susceptible to disbelief. As we can see here, Abraham was a part of that crowd. Later in the Bible, this trait of unbelief finds other victims. Some of these victims are the Lord's own disciples: People, experienced Christ here in physical presence. What more would anyone need?

I enjoy checking everything out in the Bible. You should as well. I could be stringing you along on a subject about which you know very little. You might believe every word I say.

Trusting is an admirable trait. However, in scripture we are prompted to check matters out, to see if they are according to what God has said. Taking our Bible, and reading Genesis 17:17, could be beneficial. This insight comes immediately after God spoke to Abraham concerning the coming of a son. Just look at another passage of importance, before we look at that one.

But as it is written, Eye hath not seen, nor ear heard, neither have entered into the heart of man, the things which God hath prepared for them that love him. But God hath revealed them unto us by his Spirit: For the Spirit searcheth all things, yea, and the deep things of God. 1 Cor2: 9-10

When God makes a promise, he does not take it lightly. If the promises are important to God, then they should as important to us. Every promise God makes, is so that we can have something to depend on for sure. So, when God pledges to do something, don't do what Abraham did: "Then Abraham fell upon his face, and laughed, and said in his heart, Shall a child be born unto him that is a hundred years old? And shall Sarah, that is ninety years old, bear?"

Genesis 17:17.

We do not need much of an imagination to see this picture. When I read this, it was as though I read it for the first time. I felt like bursting out with laughter too. I visualize this man of a hundred, with his face to the ground in laughter. He cannot fathom the word of God as the gospel truth in his case. I can see the tears falling from his face as he roars with a laugh of unbelief.

It seems to me as though Abe (Abraham) might just as well have voiced it like this: "Lord, it would be an easier lot to say that Ishmael is the answer to my prayer, than to expect me to believe that Sarah and I are still able to have more children."

Ishmael was the son Hagar, the servant of Sarah, Abraham's wife. This may not sound very holy in your eyes. It was not the will of God, but this is what happened when people began to take matters into their own hands. Fourteen years earlier at the age of eighty-six, Abraham figured he still had it within himself to father a child.

At the request of his wife, Abraham took her maid Hagar, and they tried to make the promise of God come true. This was not how God planned for it to happen. He had a greater and holier method with which to bring his promise to pass. God can handle these situations by himself.

Now, at the age of one hundred Abe was unable to conceive of the idea of fathering a child. I can see him visualizing Sarah, age ninety, walking around with a child in her womb. He breaks out in a torrent of laughter at the thought. When God made the promise, he purposed to keep it. The age of a man or woman would not be a deterrent.

We have taken an overview of some preparatory stages for the birth of Jacob's dad, Isaac. The name Isaac means *laughter*. Naming a child was very important then, as it is now. God named this child himself. Listen to God's response to this laughing saint: "And God said, Sarah thy wife shall bear thee a son indeed, and thou shalt call his name Isaac. " Genesis 17:19

Now, hypothetically I can see God saying: "So, nobody thinks I can do it. Watch Me."

14

God had often done miracles in the life of Abraham. It was not as though Abraham had not seen the hand of God at work; it is just that he forgot that God was always God. God does not depend on circumstances to be exactly right, to do the miraculous for those he loves.

This matter of disbelief was not a one-sided situation. Sarah faced the same problem as her hubby. Apparently, they were perfect for each other: Sarah laughed as well. Both of them soon realized that God had a greater plan in mind for them. It was something they were unable to comprehend at this time.

If we look at scripture, we will see God's declaration of confidence in the man called: "A friend of God." When God chooses someone to be of service to him, he gives them a Vote of confidence. He will place his mark upon them, so that everyone will know that they are set apart from the crowd.

I know him, that he will command his children and his household after him, and they shall keep the way of the Lord;…that the Lord may bring upon Abraham that which He hath spoken of him. Genesis 18:19.

When I really hear this with my heart, it lifts my spirit. I think of the scripture that says: "What shall we then say to these things? If God, be for us, who can be against us? He that spared not his own Son, but delivered him up for us all, how shall he not with him also freely give us all things?" Romans 8:31&32. In Genesis 21 God took care of part of that verse.

After Sarah realizes the truth of the promise of God, and realizes that their prayer is near to being answered, she says: "…God hath made me to laugh (why?), so that all that hear will laugh with me." Genesis 21:6.

Does God have a sense of humor? God named their son Isaac, *laughter*. I believe he was saying: Let this child be the joy of your old age.

I do not for a minute believe that God was being vindictive, when he named this boy *Laughter*. He was leaving Abraham and Sarah a gentle reminder about the truth of the promise: No matter how they interpreted the circumstances.

I believe that the good Lord spoke to Abraham and Sarah in the way I have inferred. If we were to put it into the vernacular of the times we are living in, I might hear it like this: "I am never going to let you forget: It is no laughing matter, when I say that a son will be born. It will happen, and Isaac is his name."

15

God does understand our frailties. He does not have to put up with us, but he loves us enough to do so. He knew from a time slot before Adam and Eve came into the picture, that we would need helps throughout the days of our lives. Our Lord never molded us with the belief that we would automatically have it together from that day forward.

God knew that from day one to day one hundred, or day two-hundred; we would need a bit of persuasion: To understand the promises he made. We never surprise God. He created us, and because of this fact, he can know how we are going to react to adverse circumstances.

Often, someone has prepared a surprise party for a friend or relative. Everyone has arrived, except the guest of honor. Someone is always elected to bring the guest, without letting him or her know where he or she is going. They usher the gullible soul into the house. Unsuspecting of what is about to happen. Suddenly, everybody is engulfed in a roar of: Surprise!

Well sometimes it is a surprise, and sometimes the gullible soul was not quite as naive as they let on.

Sometimes we mess up and think that God really did not notice. It is as though we think that we were found out because someone else had told the Lord: Like me praying and telling him that somebody else had been a naughty young woman or nasty little boy. Or, we may think that he only found out when we repented to him: Like the surprise party.

Who was there in the Garden of Eden to tell God, that Eve had eaten that which she was supposed to have been left untouched? Can I say that it was the devil? Eve told God: "The devil made me do it." (Genesis 3:13), this was her reply, because God caught her in the act.

Sarah thought she had hidden her disbelief of God's word from the Lord. The Lord asked Abraham: "…why did Sarah laugh…?" Gen.18: 13. Verse 15 is a classic example of us in our ignorance: "…I did not Laugh…" "Who, me Lord, would I laugh, when you promised me something that is impossible to do?"

I guess she thought God had not been observant enough to notice the change in her spirit. If God were not concerned, he would not likely have asked Abraham why Sarah had laughed.

During the times in which we feel that God is unable to handle our situation, we need to check out the word of God. I found a scripture that really hits home: One of those gems that we find from time to time, when we need them the most. Listen to it with me please:

16

"Is anything too hard for God?"…(Gen. 18:14a.)

It was twenty-five years from the time Abraham left Haran, to the time of the birth of his son Isaac. Within the frame this man, it seemed like a lifetime to wait for an answer to a promise.

Abraham had picked up his belongings, his family, and his future, and literally put them into the hands of God: When he left his home. From out of nowhere, God had spoken to Abraham to move on from where he was comfortable.

My sons would have been a bit disgruntled; if they'd had to wait twenty-five years for something I promised them. Whenever I have made a promise, they expected the fulfillment before nightfall. Otherwise, it seemed as if it had been an unkept promise.

Continuing to believe for something God has promised is hard: If it seems like it is never going to happen. However, time has never been a factor for God. The waiting scenario is often what God asks of us. In some ways he is saying: "I am going to do it, but you will just have to trust me on this one." He is always in control.

Waiting was going to be a trait Jacob was going to have to learn if he were to get the woman of his dreams. Before we look at Jacob, let's see what his dad was like. Isaac wanted to pass on the important things of life, to Jacob. I want to see what they are.

One entity that Abraham passed onto his son Isaacs was his human failure. He did not just pass on the ugly stuff; he also passed on a Godly legacy: Like Noah did.

Isaac Goes To School

School: Would anybody believe me if I said that this was the most exciting thing I could think of. It might be tough to believe that line.

I think of the problems that I had to face during the early years of my schooling: If I had to go back and relive them in the same way, I would consider fighting my entrance. Chances are that I would say thanks, but no thanks.

We cannot go back and change the past, if we could, we would want to change it: I am sure. When I think of Isaac in his old age, I am sure he would have tried to change the in fighting between Jacob and Esau over the family inheritance.

Controversy surrounded Isaac's birth. Ishmael was his older brother. Ishmael and Isaac were stepbrothers. Remember, the plan that Sarah had to help God's promise come to fruition.

The general practice was that the eldest son would take over the family farm. In this instance they were not going to play according to man's rules: God's law was going to reign.

Tradition had it, that the eldest son would receive the blessing from the father and receive the inheritance. God had promised the inheritance would be to the son of Abraham and Sarah: Not from a union of Abraham and Sarah's maid Hagar.

No matter how we perceive it today, it was the custom of that day, for a woman to substitute her maid for herself: if she were unable to bear children. In this way the husband could at least have children to carry on the family name.

Now that Isaac was born, Sarah became a bit concerned that Abraham may give the position of heir apparent, to the wrong person. This was not going to happen, if she could do anything about it.

It seems that Abraham may have been considering Ishmael as the heir. He might have had some reservations about his understanding of the promise of God. It may just be that he had gotten the names mixed up. Is there much difference between the name Ishmael, and Isaac? Hey, both start with the Letter "I," but they do not both have five letters. Is there a difference? You tell me.

When we read Genesis 21:9-12, we observe that Abraham evidently feels like making the switch, this is when Sarah stepped in and said: "...for the son of this bondwoman shall not be heir with my son...And the thing was very grievous in Abraham's sight because of his son...God said, let it not be grievous in thy sight,...for in Isaac shall thy seed be called."

God reaffirmed the promise made earlier. Earlier, God had made it quite clear that it was to be Isaac, not Ishmael, who would be Abraham's successor. Gen.17.18-22. Isaac vaulted into a precarious position involuntarily, when he was born. At fourteen, Ishmael might have gotten the idea that it was he, who was going to inherit the blessing from Abraham.

18

Follow me back to the old home place. Ishmael and his buddies are playing together. The proceedings get a little out of hand, he gets upset and says: "Hey people, watch out. I am going to take over when my dad dies. Then I will be your ruler. Shape up now or you will be sorry then." It is a possibility that Ishmael had already set his sights higher than he should have. He may just have had a little help from Abraham.

Abraham threw a big party for Isaac when he was old enough to eat real food, instead of mothers' milk. Ishmael looked on and began to mock Isaac. Gen. 21:9 gives us this picture.

It seems to me that Ishmael may also have begun to remember a promise that mom and dad may have talked about: The promise about Isaac being chosen to carry on dad's name. I think that Ishmael may have begun to develop a phobia, about who was going to get the right of the first-born.

Later, we will see that this was also a concern of Jacob in his dealings with his brother. I continue to find similarities that will show up as we move onto Jacob. Watch for it. The younger one displaces the oldest son.

I was hoping to say that Isaac faced the regular perplexities of life, just like the rest of us. After some thought on the matter, I realize that I have some reservations about it. Every average boy did not need to face the issue of who gets the family farm. Every average boy did not need to face the issue of who is supposed to take over the leadership role.

I look at the whole scene and think: Why would God ask Abraham to sacrifice Isaac at this time? Isaac had enough of a load to carry already, without having to carry the wood for the fire of his own execution. God was testing Abraham's willingness to obey at all costs.

At the time of this event, the age of Isaac is not clear. According to some, he was about sixteen, and according to others he may have been twenty-five. The age factor is important here. Remember that Abraham was at least 115 years old now. Isaac, being the age he was, must have had a fair amount of strength.

If the lad did not consent, it is impossible for this old man to put Isaac on the altar. Isaac was prepared to do the will of God. He already had a measure of character built up within him.

By reading chapter twenty-two of Genesis, we can readily see a submissive attitude portrayed by Isaac. Personally, I can visualize Isaac

19

saying: "I do not know what is going on here, but my dad said God told him to lay me on the altar of sacrifice: So here goes."

Has anybody noticed the traits that Abraham passed down to his son? In Gen. 12, God told Abraham to get up and go. He did not understand where exactly he was to go to, but he went anyway. I would call this submission.

I am sure that many of us are familiar with the following phrase: "The apple doesn't fall far from the tree." For the most part this is true. Then or now, seeing the character of a man or a woman passed on to their children is easy. Making sure we set proper examples is so important. Sometimes these characteristics do not surface till the children get older. Usually, similarities will surface early in one's life.

As I observe the life of Isaac, I see him as a tender person. He had a great deal of love for his mother. When she died, he felt the pain of it for about four years. It was not until he married Rebekah that he embraced any consolation.

Abraham had tenderness for the righteous people of Sodom and Gomorrah. He pleaded with God to withhold judgment. We have viewed much of the tangled life of Jacob. God is continuing to build on the initial foundations that had been set in Abraham's character. This trend will not change.

Isaac followed the tradition of his family. When his father sent him to find a wife, he obeyed. He set out and went back to Haran. It will be of particular value to remember that it was by a well that Isaac met his wife to be.

Wells can be considered as belonging to the industrious person. Anyone who has ever bought a farm has surely checked to see if it had a good well on the property. This would insure the ability to give their family the major necessities of life: After all, how far does one go without water?

Isaac was one who was engaged in the well digging business. Watch for Jacob's meeting with his prospective wife. Keep the well in your thoughts.

Preparing for Jacob is an interesting thought. Jacob was such an interesting character. The build up to his entrance needs to include some historical facts about his ancestry. I have referred to Abraham often. Until this time, I have filtered through some feelings of Isaac.

Through hardships and through the joys of life, these men had a spiritual agenda. They saw a pilgrimage on which they would be involved. To get set for Jacob and his pilgrimage, I need to do an update on the path Isaac took. I am looking forward with anticipation to my meeting with Jacob. Nevertheless, I want to let Isaac tell me a little more, of what to expect before Jacob comes on the scene.

Who is still with me?

Jacob Bergen

Are The Wells All Dug?

And Isaac digged again the wells of water, which they had digged in the days of Abraham his father; for the Philistines had stopped them after the death of Abraham: and he called their names after the names by which his father had called them. Genesis 26:18

22

Chapter 3

I have come to appreciate the value of a solid foundation. During my studies to prepare this manuscript, I knew that roots were important. If the roots of a plant or tree are rotten, it would take a considerable amount of work to salvage what, if any good there was left in the root. Not much growth is ever evident in a dry root.

When I began this chapter, I realized some harsh realities on the matter of family heritage. I have navigated much of Abraham's heritage. It is of unquestionable value. We touched a bit on the life of Isaac. His character building began in his early years. If one lives to be 180, 40 can be considered early years.

Isaac was different from both his father Abraham, and his son Jacob. His life does not appear to have the same flair as that of his predecessor. I think of him as the man in the middle.

When I think of a middleman, I see someone who will bring two sides together: Like a mediator in a labor dispute. Isaac latched onto some of what Abraham was, and connected it with Jacob. I believe that because of this, the trio could truly be all that God needed to accomplish the work of the future.

Although the bulk of Isaac's life, did not seem to include the same excitement that was noticeable in the lives of Abraham and Jacob; I see him as an equal in value, in history. It is noticeable as we look at his strengths, and yes, his weaknesses.

People like Abraham and Jacob, are generally considered the headliners of Christian history. Nevertheless, it is in the picture of Isaac, we see as a type of Christ. So tell me: "Where would you look for a foundation to lean on?"

One Sunday morning, as my wife my son, and I, were preparing to church, my son made this remark: "Dad, you really look good!" As I thought about it for a second, I looked at him and said: "You're turning out to be some kind of handsome guy yourself." After this bit of ego building he said: "I got good coaching: Just like you got from Grandpa Bergen." (My dad)

I began to marvel at the timing of God. It was this very morning that I began to write this chapter. The real life issue, which I just mentioned, revealed exactly what I have been trying to say, in preparation for the appearance of Jacob.

If I went back in time to ask Jacob of old: "To what area of your life, is your success attributed to?" I can almost hear him saying: "I got good coaching."

This pretty well says it all. Take for instance, someone who would otherwise have turned out no good: Now, come to being in a position where they turned out just fine, because of proper nourishment. I think that we all need timely helps, to give us a better chance of success.

For the next little while, let us explore the importance of wells. Whenever any tribe of people settled in a given area, they established a new well. Abraham dug wells in his day. Because of hostilities between Abraham and other nations, sometimes the enemy filled Abraham's wells with earth.

A person's well was important. Wells supplied water for the livestock, and the people. Although they said that Abraham dug wells, I would like to concentrate on the fact that Isaac also made a few excavations of this nature.

Although the following scripture does not relate to Isaac, I want to use it so that we can envision a bit of his life. It is a good idea to point out the following scripture and tack it on as a handle for Isaac:

"And the LORD shall guide thee continually, and satisfy thy soul in drought, and make fat thy bones: and thou shalt be like a watered garden, and like a spring of water, whose waters fail not. And *they that shall be* of thee shall build the old waste places: thou shalt raise up the foundations of many generations; and thou shalt be called, the repairer of the breach, the restorer of paths to dwell in." Isaiah 58:11-12

As I think about Isaac as a type of Christ, these words become rich resources. Christ came to link us with the God of our fathers: Abraham, Isaac, and Jacob. It is here, that we find our alignment to the one and only true God.

We can clearly see Isaac beginning to make a major connection with his father. Isaac was now unstopping the wells that the Philistines stopped. Beersheba became one of the most favored dwelling places of Abraham and Isaac. When I searched for a meaning, I found that Beersheba means: "The place of seven wells."

24

From what I understand from recent historical accounts, seven wells still exist at Beersheba. As I research this area, I find that a few miles of ruins litter the landscape up to the north of it. With this thought in mind I can visualize the scenery that surrounds the life of Isaac.

The ruins may not have covered the landscape then. It really doesn't matter. I am trying to compare that time with the present. I want to relate what Isaac was then, with what Christ is to us today.

The word of God tells me that Abraham planted a grove at Beersheba. In my mind, the picture is that of a peaceful place. Historical account has it that Father Abraham called on the Everlasting God here. Most of the time, he built an altar when he came to a new place.

For the most part Abraham always needed a place of communion with God. He built an altar before he roamed about in Egypt, and after he came out of that place. However, while he was in Egypt, Abraham never built an altar. Egypt was one of Abraham's greatest times of grief.

As I look at the patriarchs, I can readily see they had weaknesses: Just like those we face regularly. Though Isaac obeyed God, and did not go to Egypt, he still faced the same temptation that his father did. He lied about his wife being his sister. Lying, was a trait of those thought of as having exceptionally beautiful wives. In fact, beauty is in the eye of the beholder.

Isaac was more of a homebody. He was not as much of a traveler as his father, or his son Jacob. Maybe that is the reason he lived longer than his father, and his son. Maybe he just realized something that neither of the others did: It takes a lot less energy to stay planted, and enjoy life, than it does to be on the move and be restless. When a person stays in one place, they don't always have to be digging new wells. Their water supply usually stays in tact.

I like the definitions of the word *well*. I found the following in Roget's Thesaurus: "Source of supply, gold mine, bonanza, and resource." These words sound so inviting. I wonder if Isaac somehow knew the meaning of the word *"well?"* He may not have had a dictionary, but his chief supplier made him aware of these blessings. God appeared to Isaac and told him: "Sojourn in this land, and I will be with thee,…"Genesis 26:3

Isaac seems to have gotten a hold of that promise of provision. He let it satisfy him. If men and women today could just get a handle on that, we may have fewer problems in our world. Maybe, being satisfied with the good life is hard for us.

Peace of mind, and less of the world should be an invitation to be able to grasp. In the midst of this kind of environment, Isaac still gained great wealth. God had promised, and provided: The well (His Provision).

The Well of Provision

We face adversity more often than we care to realize. It is almost impossible to avoid. I have heard some people say that they have never faced adversity. It is not my intention to refute their statement. Nevertheless, I still believe that everyone, at some time or another, has had a time of adversity.

Maybe, at the time this person made this declaration, they have come to the point where they have learned how to handle adversity, in the way God intended. Scripture speaks of this. Hear it with me: "Don't get upset about anything, but as you pray for your needs, just be thankful for all that God has already done in the past; Then expect God to be faithful to His word again, in your present situation. Philippians 4:6, (J.B.T.)

While listening to the words, "Don't get upset," I think: How is that possible? I would say that is a reasonable thought. God's word does not change. When God assures us that everything will be okay, we need to believe it.

At some time, and in some manner, we are supposed to get a handle on that issue. As we continue to read that verse, we can hear the means by which we can accomplish this. Prayer and petition are some keys to success.

The Bible also makes it a prerequisite that we are to make these requests with thankful hearts. If we have this attitude, this intent as our goal, then God will give us something to replace the thing that has been the problem in our lives. I see something else in the passage of scripture in Philippians: The writer is telling us to give God a present.

I put myself in the scenario of being the subject of a kingdom, and receiving an invitation to the birthday party of my King. When I come to the party, I would bring him a gift of some kind. His approval is the most important thing on my mind as I approach the throne. My gift is presented to Him on my knees.

We have all seen enough movies to be able to picture the scene in our mind. As we wait for him to open our present, we do so with anticipation. When he finally opens it, a smile appears on his face. It is at this juncture that I, for one, am relieved. Now I know that my gift pleased him.

In the verse we are looking at, I can see this picture: I can see us walking down the aisle, and giving God our fears and frustrations as a gift. I can see our Heavenly Father smiling, and saying thanks as He receives our presentation.

Another relevant portion of scripture in relationship to this subject is this: "Cast all your cares (fears, anxiety) on him, because He does care for you."1 Peter 5:7.

As we get back to Isaac, I recall something I eluded too earlier. The loss of his mother Sarah, has deeply affected Isaac. Read Genesis 24:67 with me: "Isaac was comforted after his mother's death."

A period of about four years separated the death of Sarah and the marriage of Isaac to Rebekah. During this time it appears that Isaac suffered much, because of the passing of his mom. When Isaac began to love Rebekah, he finally let go the hurt of losing his mother.

The story surrounding the meeting of Isaac and Rebekah is definitely archaic. It was an arranged marriage. The father of the groom sent his servant to find a wife for his son. Ever wonder what may have happened if your dad had sent someone to find a wife or a husband for you? It is an interesting thought.

In some respects, we may see some merit to the idea of the choice of a mate being made for us. Here, they did not base the choice, on superficial characteristics such as beauty. It was very important for the chosen one to be from the right family. While the process of selection took place, the strength of the woman was considered very important. She needed to be strong enough to carry water from the well.

I do not think that the servant of Abraham (Eleizer) was so much interested in whether or not she was the local beauty pageant queen. Great importance is placed on the need for the woman to be of a good background: If in the overall picture, she was to be the mother of nations of people.

The servant went and did as his master had requested him to do. He traveled back to the same area in which Abraham had first settled after his exodus from Ur. The servant goes on to capture the heart of a young woman.

It is one thing to capture the heart of a person for yourself, yet an entirely different one to entice her to come back to marry your friend. This is tantamount to what is considered a blind date. Some of us can relate to that kind of situation. It might have been good, or it may have been like a bad dream.

With Isaac, it was not a situation where he had a bad dream: At least not for some years. What I am insinuating, is that he may have had some reservations later, when Rebekah and Jacob perpetrated one of the biggest scams of all time.

I am alluding to the time when Jacob stole his brother's birthright (inheritance). Much of this book will reveal itself from that point on. The central issue that I want to reflect on as I end this chapter is this:

Isaac's Well of Provision

Anxiety is a subject matter I referred to earlier. Sometime before that, I also referred to the fact that Isaac was not a traveler to the extent that his father was. Nor, did he trek as many miles as Jacob did.

Apparently he waited for the timing of God to look after the need he had. The need he had was that of getting something to console him for the loss of his mother. Think back to the scenario we just looked at, where we were giving our anxiety to God as a gift.

The provision, which he received from God, was the gift of having Rebekah presented to him. He could literally hang onto this provision. This did not mean that everything would be cookies and ice cream for time and eternity. We are going to see that later. Nevertheless, what it does mean is that God looked after Isaac's biggee (his greatest need at the time).

In the recess of my mind I see Father Abraham having sensed the hurt of his son, and in a spirit of compassion he says to his servant: "Go find consolation for my boy."

The name Rebekah does not mean consolation, though I may wish it did. In fact it means, a rope, or a noose. Maybe that will become apparent as we see her down the road, at another place, and another time. We can glean portions for our lives, as we go on with our subject title: JACOB!

I believe that no matter how unpopular the preacher, book, or religious personality may be, we can always find something of value. Many may recall having heard the saying, "One man's garbage is another man's gold." As I write this manuscript, I am finding gems for myself. If only I come to a closer relationship with God, then this book has filled the bill.

We have only just begun to scratch the surface of this book. We are still in the stages of looking at the reasons why Jacob was what he was: By this I do not mean we should only cover his bad points. The life of Jacob includes much more than deception.

Deception was not his best side. In the end we might have to agree in saying: Jacob's best suit was love. I see that Jacob cared deeply for his family. Oh, we will see many mistakes that he made, but that only makes him human: Like us.

In the next chapter we will explore more of the ladies' part of the picture. Sometimes, I ladies must read books by men and think: Only men in the Bible were important to God. Much of what was in Isaac, and Jacob, and a host of others as well, came from the mother's side of the ledger.

This should be interesting: The man looking through the eyes of the woman: Well, maybe just trying. Let's find out together how it turns out. Can you take it men? Are you ready ladies?

I am about to raise the curtain!

Don't leave your seats!

Presenting The Ladies

And it came to pass, when he was come near to enter into Egypt, that he said unto Sarai his wife, Behold now, I know that thou art a fair woman to look upon. Genesis 12:11

And they blessed Rebekah, and said unto her, Thou art our sister, be thou the mother of thousands of millions, and let thy seed possess the gate of those which hate them. Genesis 24:60

Chapter 4

Act One

When we consider the word mankind, we must recognize the fact that it means men and women, boys and girls. It looks to me like everybody is included, in the word mankind. We cannot have one without the other.

In the order of creation, God created the man first. This does not mean that he was more important, it only means that God put things in a certain order. The picture of order is quite evident in the creation of earth. The Bible tells us that the earth was without form, and void. It was dark. One of God's first commandments was: "Let there be light."

Putting things in proper order is much easier if I can see where they are to be placed. I will imagine for a moment that I am a librarian. My task is to arrange a massive array of books on shelves. Not only, do I need to place them on shelves, but they are to be placed in alphabetical order. Although it may take some time, I think that I can handle the job.

Now, here is the assignment with a few conditions added. Condition number one: It has to be done after midnight. Condition number two: It will be done in the dark. The reason for this is that the city has experienced a power failure. The final request is, that by morning the task is to be complete. I know that my response would be something like this: "Thanks, but no thanks. You'll have to find yourself another boy."

I realize that God could have created everything, without the use of light of any kind. However, God did create us to need light to carry out certain tasks. God shows us order, so that we can learn to live effectively. I am speaking about the man that surfaced first, by God's design.

The record of the Bible shows us that in the periscope of time, someone special would appear. Jesus Christ is that person. Not only, was He scheduled to appear, but in time, His task was to begin to prepare a bride, (the church) a lady.

At the beginning God created: heaven, earth, the balance of creation, and man. God knew that the man would be lonely if he had no companion: So he brought the lady onto the scene. God never intended the two to be two, but one. It was to be a combined entity: Just like the man Christ Jesus, and the church (His bride).

31

Writing a book on Christ and the bride (the church), and all the matters of why the order of things is important, would probably be easy. That is not my intent in this book. I have only tried to show a little bit of how having order is important. Ladies, please do not feel unimportant, because God made man first.

One scripture that I know would even lend credence to being created second. It may be a little out of context here, but I will risk it: "Nevertheless, many that are first will be last; and the last shall be first." Matt. 19:31.I will use this passage as one to give encouragement to the ladies. They also have a role to play in God's order of things, along with the man.

It may appear as though I am chasing rabbits in the early portion of this chapter, please forgive me this time. My intention is to set the stage, so that people will notice the entrance of the ladies for what it is: One of the most important things God created. Laying the groundwork for building a complex is essential. Setting the props for a stage production is also vital.

When God had finished creating the world and everything in it, He sat back and said it was very good. God then placed that lovely creation, the woman, into the picturesque garden. As He placed her beside the man, I see the man saying: Wow!

As she begins to focus her eyes after her arrival, Eve sees Adam. Let us allow ourselves to use a bit of the vocabulary of our day, and insert it into the mouth of this first lady. If we do that, we may hear these startling words: "WHAT A HUNK!"

All of us have probably been around long enough to handle that line. We can take it, can't we?

Personally, I have been around long enough to have over heard a few remarks by both men and women: Remarks that may shock some of you. I have seen the eyes of a man pop out at the sight of a physically attractive lady.

My observational receivers (my eyes) have also noted the ladies responding with words that may shock a few men. The picture in my mind is this: The Garden of Eden is presented as a beauty pageant. Eden is the place where God presented His best to us. Placing the heritage of Jacob in this context is beneficial for me.

Considerable detail has already been articulated, about Abraham and Isaac. The character of Jacob, or for that matter, that of our own started in the Garden of Eden. It did not begin with Abraham and Isaac. If we were to look at history in this light, we would see much more than the surface revelations of people.

Most of the time when a child is born people are trying to figure out: Who in the world it looks like. People usually say: "It looks like the mother, or it looks like the father." We have all heard people say: "The child looks like the parent, or the grandparent."

It is a sure bet, that a baby's looks can be entrusted to him or her through birth. We can be sure that the traits of the parents are inbred as well. Children are not carbon copies; they develop some individual characteristics.

The point I would like to make is this: Jacob did not only get all his good and bad characteristics, from Abraham and Isaac alone. A couple of ladies, whom they knew, had some participation.

Enter: Sarah & Rebekah

Sarah was Jacob's grandmother. From all the scriptures that I find in Genesis, I understand her to be a woman that would turn a few heads. Abraham told her that she was beautiful. I wonder if he told her very often. One instance, in which he told her that she was beautiful, was when he needed a favour. He needed her to tell a little white lie.

When Abraham went to Egypt, he was afraid that Sarah's beauty would turn the Pharaoh's head, and possibly cost him his head. When I read chapter 12 of Genesis, I realize that Sarah must have complied with Abe's wishes. I see here that she was a woman that he could depend upon, when the chips were down. I would say that she stood by her man.

It is evident to me, as we look at life, that many times this characteristic of a woman made the marriage relationship a good one. It was not because the woman cowered in the presence of her man; she honoured God in this manner. In a good relationship, this action of a woman also causes the man to respect a woman. Now, we have at least one picture of a relationship where the two people become one.

On the other side of this issue, we find adverse results: Where men and women do not respect each other. The world is full of examples of this type of relationships as well. The key elements to success require a bit of cooperation from both parties. Someone has to make the first move.

I realize, that to often it has been the lady who has had to show her hand first. I believe that this is one of the finest qualities that God has placed within the heart of women. A woman, who can accept a role such as this, is number one for sure.

The Bible tells us that the man is to be the head of the home, as Christ is the head of the church (Bride, lady). Reading it from Ephesians 5, is imperative at this point. Before going any further, take special note of the later part of the chapter, from verse 21-33.

In order for both men and women to see their proper role of conduct, reference essential. One thing for both men and women to realize is that neither position is superior, or inferior.

Abraham was a man who realized that working together was beneficial. When he was concerned for his life at the hands of Pharaoh, he did not command Sarah to lie for him: He asked her to do it. I think she did it because she loved him. She spoke her mind when she felt that doing so was necessary. (See Genesis 16).

In the culture of Biblical times, being childless left a mark on the character of a woman. Being childless was not a comfortable position to be in. Sarah felt the sting of this embarrassment for many years. She should not have been in despair about it. God had promised to give her a child. Sarah should have remembered the old matter of trusting that God would deliver the goods: Which He promised to deliver.

Well, Sarah devised a plan that would cause the birth of a child for her hubby. It would not be hers, but at least Abraham would have a child to carry on the family name. That was the key to the whole matter. A son had to be born to Abraham. Any other plan was no good.

The problem that arose was this: Sarah did not consult God about the matter. Sarah had gotten a wrong number. Though Sarah's heart was in the right place, a problem existed with what Sarah had done. She did not want Abraham to look bad among his peers. This is the admirable trait that I observe. The name Sarah means: Princess.

Princess is a name that gives one a sense of dignity. Imagine for a moment, Abraham coming home from a hard day out on the field. He walks into the tent and he sees Sarah. He could see her as just plain Jane, or he could see her as a princess. If he saw her as a princess, she could have him eating out of her hand.

I see a bit of a parallel in the fact of Sarah having her name changed from Sari, to Sarah (princess). The parallel I see, is in what Jacob had his name changed to. Jacob went from being a deceiver to: *PRINCE WITH GOD.*

I find no record for what the name Sari means: But in my sometimes-bent way of trying to sort things out, I wonder if it did not mean, deceiver. Sarah was manipulative in the way she tried to help God.

What happened was, that Sarah gave her servant to her husband: So that he could have a child by her. It was common practice in those days for this to happen. It was after this affair that Abraham got his name: It used to be Abram. It was also after this affair that Sari became Sarah: Princess.

When I use the word affair, I do not mean for it to sound like an act of immorality. Hagar, Sarah's maid, became a wife of Abraham. This meant that she now would have to share the relationship she had with her husband.

Sarah must have been a bit naive to think her maid would still be meek and mild after she gave birth: When she could not conceive for her own husband. Hagar wasted little time to rub it in the face of Sarah. Sarah had some clout in her relationship with Abe. When she laid out the problem to her husband, he said: "Do what you have to do to give yourself peace of mind over the issue."

Well Sarah did just that. She just made it unbearable for her maid to stick around. As a result, Hagar leaves home. Later Hagar came back at the request of God. In due process, Sarah did conceive the promised child.

Again, the issue of the other woman and her son presented itself. Again, Sarah threw her weight around. She had the woman kicked out. Tell me; does that sound as if Sarah were meek and mild? I don't think so! She had a deep regard for her husband; she also spoke up when she had a problem with a given situation.

It is almost unbelievable, how God could take a person who is so self willed and unkind at times, and say: *Come here Princess, I love you.* If that were not in the heart of God, I cannot see him calling her princess: Can you?

Sarah had beauty and charm, and honoured others. She was self willed and cruel, and a whole lot of other things as well. Keep her at the forefront of your thoughts as we continue. See how many of those similarities Sarah transferred to Jacob.

Watch closely for every possible connection. The purpose of history is to allow us to make connections with the past. We are compiling a considerable amount of history from which to learn.

Sarah is about to leave the set. Nevertheless, before she does, hear this. "Listen to me, you who pursue righteousness and who seek the Lord: Look to the rock from which you were cut and to the quarry from which you were hewn; Look to Abraham, your father, and to Sarah, who gave you birth. When I called him he was but one, and I blessed him and made him many." Isaiah 5: 1&2.

In this short passage I see a vivid, full-length novel. I see that looking back at our roots is important. Nobody is here just to look out for himself or herself. We are all individual in many ways, but that is something that can cause us to impart something of value into someone else's life.

Sarah's name is mentioned with the same importance as that of Abraham. Scripture also goes on to say that out of this union, they built nations. From beginning to end, we all fit together into a gigantic picture puzzle. We are of no value as individual pieces of that puzzle.

I could have elaborated on many other things regarding Sarah. Nevertheless, I think we can pick up some of those things in her daughter-in-law. We do not want to pass over another important lady.

I consider the ladies in the Bible, as important as the men of the Bible. Many of these women would enhance the scene that we are painting. Because of the subject I am dealing with, I will only include two of them at this point. One of these ladies of distinction has already played some of her parts. Her name was Sarah, "Princess."

Act Two

Another lady of distinction that I would like to take a serious look at is Rebekah. As we observe some of her life, we will also look at the meaning of her name. The pictures displayed in the meaning of her name are quite interesting. Nevertheless, before we go on to explore those avenues in the life of Rebekah, we should observe what she was like when she first entered the scene.

I am going to set up some props here on the stage of life. Someone once said: "The world is a stage." If this is the case, we need some props to illustrate the scenes. On the platform of the set, I am placing a grove of trees around a well. Along with the well, is an assortment of animals. To finish off the scene, I have reinforced the set with some people. Some of them are busy drawing water, while others are just lazily conversing with one another.

After looking around for a time, I sense that most of the folks are locals. It appears that others may be travellers from afar. One such traveller is a man who has quite a convoy of camels and men in his party. As he approaches the well, he does so with an air of expectancy. The man in question is the servant of Father Abraham. His orders are to retrieve a certain woman to be the wife of his son Isaac.

When I take a close look at the traveller, I see a look of concern on his face, as to whether or not he can fulfill the request of his master. He is concerned enough to ask God to guide him to the right young lady. At first glance he cannot seem to find anyone who he considers to be a contender for the position of takeout bride for his Master's son.

As he stands there trying to look inconspicuous, Eliezer sees a young lady approaching the well, to fill her pitchers with water. Her approach is kind of in a hop, skip, and a jump attitude. She is carefree and happy in her appearance.

Not quite knowing whom to approach at first, Abraham's servant waits for a considerable amount of time. Because of the fact that he was away from his home territory, it was imperative that he should be careful with which young woman he made conversation. It is a possibility that this young lady at the well, may be seriously connected to one the men gathered around the well.

37

Nevertheless, after this young woman had drawn sufficient water for her needs, Abraham's servant decides to make his pitch. He approaches her and says, "Please let me have a little water from your pitcher."

It was a simple request. Rebekah could have answered it in any one of several ways. Upon hearing the man's plea for water, she said: "Drink my lord,…I will get water for your camels too, till they have finished drinking."

Now, this is exactly the reply that the servant was hoping to hear. Rebekah must have surveyed the situation for at least a moment, before she said: Come to my father's house, Rebekah was a young lady who was eager to please. It appears to me as though she was willing to go the extra mile to help someone. She had an excellent attitude. I am not so sure that all the women were just that eager to satisfy a perfect stranger. Nevertheless, this young person had been set apart at the request of Abraham's servant.

Let us recall the time when God told Abraham to get up and go into a land that was yet unknown to him. The man picked up his baggage and went. I see something special about our lady in waiting. It shows me a willingness to obey, in the same way that Abraham did.

The stage is set with Rebekah, her brother and other family members. The meeting-taking place revolves around the issue of Rebekah returning with Abraham's servant: To become the bride of his son. Picture yourself in this scenario. Someone says: *Do* you want to go on a blind date?

My initial thought concerning a blind date would be, "What is my chance of a good catch?" I am not only referring to looks when I say this. Some people just do not hit it off together. In a flash of daring, responding with a quick yes might be easy.

Apprehension is one thing I would struggle with, while I went through the stages of preparation. I would wonder: Will this be my dream come true? When I put my imagination to work, it is easy to see some thoughts that were going through the mind of Rebekah. Finally, the men around the fire call Rebekah, and ask her this question:" Will you go with this man?"

I am beginning to notice a touch of daring in Rebekah. Maybe I could call it that measure of faith. She gives an immediate response. "I will go."

Rebekah was still young and innocent. She was flirtatious with what life had to offer. I think she was excited at the thought of exploring the unseen. Maybe she had the same measure of the faith that Abraham had at the beginning.

I do not know if she asked a whole lot of searching questions about all that would happen if she went. What I see is a readiness to comply when God calls. So far, Rebekah has positively impressed me.

Until this point in time, we have seen some of these same characteristics in Sarah. Beauty, gentleness, kindness, and a host of other good things, were a part of Rebekah's makeup. She is from a well to do family. She had a nurse, and maids.

When Rebekah arrived at the destination that had been arbitrarily charted for her, she laid eyes on her blind date. As she approaches the man that she has come all this way to marry, Rebekah covers her face in a display of modesty. We can visualize what it must have been like.

Much of what I write is based on how it might have been in real life back then. As I write about people and life then, I try to compare it with the mind-set of people in our culture. Every detail of a person's thoughts and intentions is not made clear in the Bible.

Many issues represented in Old Testament times are the same as those we face today. The words may have been different, but I think the feelings within were much the same. We need to reset the props on the stage of life from time to time.

On one side of the giant stage I see a field, hills, and the sight of a man focussing on something approaching his domain. On the other side of the set, we have some camels, men and women, and an assortment of items, which are stowed by a person on the move.

Two people with high expectations about each other are about to meet. Everything in the whole scene has been left up to the stagehands to arrange. A servant, of all people, managed the whole set.

The decisive moment has arrived, and the man of the hour is Isaac. The lady in waiting is Rebekah. When Isaac sees her, I can see him running out to his servant and saying: "Man, you did a good job!"

Try to paint a picture of what Becky is thinking. It may sound like this: "Yea, this guy is not so bad!" Admitting these kinds of thoughts aloud might not have been proper, for fear of being looked upon badly. These thoughts do exist in the mind of many people.

By looking at the story in the Bible, (Genesis 24) we will see this to be the case. Here we can get all the details. The space to tell every part of the story that has relevance to this account of history is unavailable to me. Maybe I could call it: *Her story*, rather than His *story* (history).

I have seen many admirable things in the character of our star. She may be the woman of everybody's dreams. She has distinctly captured the heart of the co-star, Isaac.

In the closing scene of this production, I want to see how powerfully affected this man of historical significance was: At the hands of the lovely lady. As we raise the curtain for the final scene of act two, we see a wedding taking place. Laughter, and merry making are the dominant scenes, but the story line is set back in a corner.

Apart from the exuberance of the moment, I see another scene depicted. I see a man and a woman, embraced in true love. I am talking about something other than an act of immorality. As they look into each other's eyes, I can literally feel the love they share. What Rebekah was to Isaac, is hard to put into words.

As the curtain begins to fall, I read these words: "And Isaac brought her into his mother Sarah's tent, and took Rebekah, and she became his wife, and he loved her: and Isaac was comforted after his mother's death." Gen.24: 67.

Earlier on, I said that I wanted to look at what the name Rebekah meant. She did not have her name changed, as did Sarah. Recall with me that Sarah's name meant *"Princess."* The word Rebekah means *" a rope, or noose."*

Initially, these words sound harsh to me. The tough phrase, *"a rope, or noose"* leads me to envision someone who captures another with his or her beauty. Rebekah had a way that attracted people. It happened at the well when the servant was searching for a wife for Isaac, and it happened when Isaac first saw the one who was to be his wife.

I am not going to elaborate on the words that describe her name right now. I have got a reason to keep this for another portion in the book. So watch for it later.

Give me the power to attach a meaning to the name Rebekah: Let my temptation finish the task, and I will say the name Rebekah means: Comforter.

At this stage in her life, she literally became comfort in a human body, for a person who was in need. Isaac was a man in serious need during this time. Rebekah will also prove to have a darker side to her character: As it seems many of us do. She will play an integral part in the life of Jacob.

Come with me now, as we meet the children born in this union of love.

Jacob Bergen

Part Two

?

Who Gets The Family Farm

Jacob Bergen

Two For The Promise

For the promise is unto you, and to your children, and to all that are afar off, *even* as many as the Lord our God shall call. Acts 2:39

Jacob Bergen

Chapter 5

At this juncture of the book, I have tried to revolve mostly around people who contributed to the life of Jacob: Before he was even born. Always, these were people who gave Jacob inherent character. This being the case is not sufficient reason to place all the blame on others, for things that may be character flaws.

Though the blood relationship to others affects some facets of our lives, we still have a responsibility to follow the guidelines outlined in the road map. Sometimes I hear people say: "The devil made me do it," when caught in the act of wrongdoing.

It is likely that we all know someone who has used this phrase, for an excuse to get off the hook. I realize, that sometimes people have inherited a physical problem, because of some parent's disability.

Easy cures do not accompany some of these afflictions. Many have no cures. Our hereditary, is not always easy to deal with. However, we can deal with them, if we are seriously willing to let God will prevail.

We have heard the saying, "Love covers a multitude of sins." It is true. Love may cover most sins: But it does not erase them. Right now I am only speaking of human love. We cannot guarantee that the physical act of love bears perfect children. The act of love may have been done in perfect love: But the inherent imperfection of our ancestry, restrains us from being able to assure anyone that we will have perfect children.

One couple, in very close relationship to my wife and me, had a set of twins. Just for the record, they were twin boys. They were born very much prematurely. They were only one and three-quarter lbs. and two lbs. three-quarter ounces respectively, at birth.

Because of their size, they faced many problems in their early days of childhood. Perfection did not show itself as present in their lives. They began to grow, and are really quite healthy now, but they are still not perfect. They are very much like any growing child. If someone implied that about my child I would have to agree. Oh, I could easily say that I loved them, and they were good children all right, but perfect, not a chance.

Like many other parents these were also proud as punch at the arrival of their children. They made up a birth announcement that read in part as follows:

Howling Success I & Howling Success II

Although they were identical twins, one of them had to be the first to arrive on the scene. One of them arrived at 5:01 A.M., while the other made his debut at 5.05 A.M.

These boys have often been a pleasure to us. We can sit back and see how some traits they display, resemble the parents. One boy has more of his mother's characteristics, while the other leans a bit more to the characteristics of his father. This is a profile of real life, as it exists today.

I have related this true account to reflect upon another real life experience that took place sometime ago: In fact it was well over three thousand years ago. I think that I will tag this scene with a headline. Let's call it:

A Howling Success

Isaac and his bride of twenty years were an important part of world events. Had there been a newspaper in those days, it would likely have read:

HEIR APPARENT FINALLY ARRIVES.

Under the headline, they may have scribed these words:
"Successors are born to a patriarch of Israel. After what seems like eternity, his wife was finally able to have children. Nobody really knows for sure why they did not have children before this. People have suggested various reasons for this dilemma, but they can attribute no validity to any of the hearsay.

It is usually a happy day when that which they expected finally arrives. In this couple, Isaac and Rebekah, it is a case of: Double your pleasure; Double your fun. You guessed it. They have twins.

This could present a problem down the road, when it is time to decide who is number one. Two heirs are presented, to take up one position. The boys' names are Esau, and Jacob. According to this reporter's research the name Esau, "means hairy," while the name Jacob, "means supplanter."

Well so long for now.

This Is The Nose in Everybody Else's Affairs, For The Daily Gossip, Signing Off For Now.

Sometimes I wonder why they give people certain names. My name is Jacob: Because my parents named me after my grandfather. I can understand why they named Esau what they did: It was because of his birth the features. He was reddish, and hairy. Esau headed a race of people called Edomites. The word Edom means red, maybe his nickname was Red.

Something that has puzzled me is the fact that Isaac and Rebekah gave Jacob that name: Without someone else in the family line having had that name. This was the first Jacob of the Bible. In fact, I can only find one other Jacob in the Bible. This also represents a first. This Jacob is the first in the New Testament. He was the father of Joseph, the husband of Mary, the mother of Jesus.

The word Jacob means the supplanter. Many words could best describe the word to supplant. I find definitions such as: Act for, pinch hit, relieve, crowd out, displace, and stand in the stead of: These are just some definitions I found. Some of them have extreme implications.

Why would anybody tag a child with handles like that? They have not even had a chance to give us those impressions of themselves. The word, supplant, also has the meaning to replace, succeed, and supersede. In this context they do not sound as severe.

If we supplanted someone under these conditions, it would be more as though it may be a power gain of natural succession. It would not seem as one that was perpetrated in deception: The way the other definitions seem to imply.

When I began to try to figure out this dilemma, I also began to realize some things in life that are important. Isaac, and Rebekah must have known who was talking to them. God spoke to Abraham and Sarah in the same way that He spoke to Isaac, and Rebekah. Nevertheless, at that point they thought they had to make it happen their way.

Isaac and Rebekah decided that they had waited long enough. After twenty years it was time to do something about their childlessness. Now was not the time to take second best. It was time to pray. This is precisely what Isaac did. In answer to prayer his wife became expectant.

When we do right, right episodes begin to develop in our lives. When God spoke to Cain, He said: "If you will do the things that are right, will you not be accepted?" Genesis 4:7

Abraham had faith in God when he first met him. Why didn't he have faith enough when it was time for the promised child to arrive? Maybe he did not understand what God meant, though he spoke to him as plainly as he did to Isaac and Rebekah.

I see that Isaac and Rebekah must have had a tremendous amount of faith, when they named the second of the twins Jacob (supplanter). Listen to the words God spoke to them:

"Two nations are in your womb, and two peoples from within you will be separated; one people will be stronger than the other, and the older will serve the younger." Gen.25: 23. They literally took God's word and said: "Okay, we will call the second twin Jacob because he is going to stand in place of Esau, the first born."

This mom and dad virtually saw the word of God as already done at this time. Later, we will see that they did not always remember with clarity what God had said the first time. Anyway, Isaac seemed to have forgotten.

The position of being the oldest in a family was very important. I saw a portrayal of this with Abraham and Sarah. As Abraham saw it, Ishmael was born first. Though Abraham did not conceive the boy through a union of himself and his first wife Sarah, Ishmael was the first-born son of Abraham.

I have already dealt with this issue, so I will not dwell on it. I only want to say that in the eyes of Abraham, Ishmael was entitled to the birthright (right of the oldest in the family).

It is easy to see how conflict could arise in this family. Not only is it evident between the boys, but between the parents as well. Depending from which side of the picture we approach the matter, everybody could be right.

The traditional way was that the eldest son legally had the right to take over the family farm, after dad was out of the picture. We need to remember that God never promised the birthright to Abraham and Hagar, but to Abraham and Sarah. This is what God said, not what tradition inferred.

When it came time for Isaac to get married, Abraham sent his oldest servant to find a wife for Isaac. Here it is again, the oldest is chosen for the important task. Now, coming back to Esau and Jacob, Esau was the first to arrive, with Jacob hot on his heels. Hypothetically speaking, I see Jacob saying: "I am hanging onto your heel's Esau. You are not going without me."

By looking at this scenario, it almost seems as if Jacob knew that he was to be the heir to the farm.

Jacob was hanging onto the heels of Esau for dear life. (Gen. 25:26) It is ironic, that in most every case people have memory lapses, concerning what God said at the beginning.

If we begin to take notes of the proceedings in the early years in the boys' lives, we will see that Isaac begins to favour Esau: While Rebekah begins to value Jacob more than his brother.

I get the impression that Isaac began to think of Esau as the heir apparent. Not only is this my impression, but scripture also confirms this. (Gen. 27:4,33, &37). These passages tell me that Isaac had expected to give the birthright to Esau, because he was angry when he found out that Jacob had taken it by devious means.

According to the historical account, it appears that Esau was a hard-core man. He was a hunter and he caught the eyes of his father. Jacob on the other hand was more inclined to help mom in the kitchen. Maybe in the early years dad would say, "Come on boys, let's go hunting." Maybe Esau was eager and ready, while Jacob said, "Sorry dad, I'll have to take a rain check. I am in the middle of a batch of cookies."

Picturing how Isaac would become more enamoured with Esau is easy. From time to time one of my sons has asked me to go fishing. I have usually said no, I have too many chores on my list. A couple of times excuses may be acceptable. If every time he asks me, I have an excuse, he will soon stop asking me to fish with him. He will think I just don't like fishing: So why try to force me.

51

I can also see how mom would get to appreciate Jacob more than Esau. Jacob was willing to help her in the kitchen, while Esau just wanted to get out of the house with his bow and take down a deer. The problems in this home began in the early stages. Both husband and wife had differing views about who was number one.

When the time comes for Isaac to die, a position for the leadership of Israel would be open. Only one man can do the job. The unique thing about it was that the job was not up for bids. God had already foretold the results.

The problem arose, when one parent did not keep their eyes focussed on what God had said at the beginning. I am quite aware of the difficulty involved in trying to change the tradition of another person. After all, the oldest is the only candidate: Isn't he?

We have the same problem with a host of other matters in our Christian walk. We stumble along wondering why we face so many hardships. When someone says, "If you did what God said to do, your problem would not exist", we are ready to scrap. My reply goes as follows: "It is not as easy as you think," and it isn't.

God made one promise, and wanted only one ruler for this family. We never see two kings ruling one country. It is always one king at a time.

When I see two children in a royal family, one will become the heir to the throne, while the other will serve as a subject of that heir. I can sympathize with Esau. I see him saying: "It is not fair. It is supposed to be my kingdom, not yours Jacob." In a herd of wild horses, the stallions fight for the position of king of the hill.

Think through with me on this next thought. What if, when God said, "Two nations are in thy womb, and two manner of people shall be separated from the bowels; and the one people shall be stronger than the other people, and the elder shall serve the younger," He was only saying it to let them know how it was going to happen: Not necessarily saying that this is how he wanted it to be.

What if God really wanted it to be done in the traditional manner: But it could not turn out that way because Esau did not respect the position of leadership he thought was his for the taking. He did not really think it was all that important, till he lost it. This is just one of my: "What if thoughts."

Remember when Sarah had a concern that Ishmael might get the position belonging to Isaac: God told Abraham to listen to his wife, because she had it figured right.

God said: "...my covenant will I establish with Isaac,..."Gen.17: 21 and, "...in Isaac shalt thy seed be called." Gen. 21:12

When God said, "My covenant shall be with Isaac," Isaac was not yet born. God was in effect, naming him right then. I do not find this to be the case when the twins were born. Then God said: "Two nations...in thy womb. The older shall serve the younger."

At this point God did not say, "In Jacob shall thy seed be," or "My covenant shall be in Jacob." God did not name Jacob before he was born. He had to do it afterwards. God would give Jacob his proper name after he had come to know who God really was. God was Jacobs spiritual Father, the One who would bless him with a greater inheritance.

Now I see that God only let Isaac and Rebekah know what was going to happen: Just like someone predicting your future. When someone predicts our future, we can make sure that it does not happen that way. When God foretells our future, we have no way of changing it.

Esau had the choice of reaching out for the birthright. When he should have reached out for the fulfilment of his spiritual needs, he chose to have his physical need met. After this, Jacob and his mother did everything in their power to make sure that Esau could not renege on his part of the agreement.

Isaac also tried to change what God had foretold. I don't know if he did it intentionally, thinking God had made a mistake, but he tried. If we look at the Bible thoroughly, we can look at both sides of the same coin. Nevertheless, only one side will come up. Which will it be?

Well, families are an interesting lot. Times are, when the good times surround us. Then when we least expect it, the bad times come to the surface of the waters. Some come out winners, while the others may be the losers.

We have only just begun to touch on the subject of Jacob. Along with him, there is going to be a host of other interesting folk.

Stick with me now, and I will display a real life rip off.

The Big Scam

This twenty years have I been with thee; thy ewes and thy she goats have not cast their young, and the rams of thy flock have I not eaten. That which was torn of beasts I brought not unto thee; I bare the loss of it; of my hand didst thou require it, whether stolen by day, or stolen by night˙ Thus I was; in the day the drought consumed me, and the frost by night; and my sleep departed from mine eyes˙ Thus have I been twenty years in thy house; I served thee fourteen years for thy two daughters, and six years for thy cattle: and thou hast changed my wages ten times. Genesis 31:38-41

Chapter 6

As I write, I try to set up windows through which we can reflect on the past. While in these window frames, I try to insert small focus points to show what I am going to embrace in detail later.

This is similar to computer software. While working in my workstation on a certain subject, I often have to go through windows to look for helps to complete my task. When the necessary information is found, I can easily insert it into the file on which I am working.

As we are surveying this subject, I find no immediate value in simply saying that Jacob did this, that, or the other. If I simply talk exclusively about him page after page, without reference to the people, places, and interests surrounding him, we would have no story.

From time to time I have to go back through a window type system, in the framework of my mind. I do this to bring out subject matter that will highlight a matter important for that particular moment.

In the previous chapter, I began to allude to the fact that there was a bit of a separation taking place in the family of Becky and Ike. As time went on we saw favouritism being displayed. Maybe mom would bake Jacob his favourite pie, as a show of her special love for him. On the other side of the picture, I could see how dad might have spent some quality time fashioning a new bow, and a set of arrows specially crafted for Esau.

Circumstances of this nature are not clearly illustrated in the Bible. However, favouritism was evidently practised. What better way is there to express it, than to do special niceties for the person we favour. These acts of special favour seemed to have begun with Isaac.

At the time of birth, all he could think about was: "Will my wife give me a son?" When the first child graces this world with its presence, I see a man filled with joy and fulfilment. From a full heart he might have expelled words like:

"It's a boy. It's a boy!"

The start of special status for Esau his firstborn, was at the forefront of his mind. Being the first-born gave him this special right. I can almost visualize Isaac bestowing the blessing on his son at that point.

I suspect that Esau felt that he did not have to worry much about his rights. He seemed to have dad eating out of his hand. It was as if he could go out at anytime, and bring home the big buck.

The word of God informs me that Ike loved deer meat. Apparently Esau had a special way to prepare this dish that captured the appetite of his father. Esau had the knack for pleasing his dad. I guess this cannot hurt when you're in line to get the goods. God told Isaac and Rebekah that in time, Esau would not end up receiving the right of birth.

Esau did not know about that word from God. So, it was just natural for him to take for granted that there was not a problem in the works. When I search out the word of the Lord concerning the twins, it seems as if Esau did not even have time to eat, once he went out on the hunt. It was so much apart of him that it was all that he could think about. On one such occasion he nearly starved to death before he came to his senses, and came home to eat.

By putting all his efforts into his enjoyment of the great outdoors, Esau put himself into a precarious position. His addiction, rather than being focussed on his need clouded his judgement.

We all need proper balance in every area of our lives. When we observe a balanced lifestyle, then our decision-making skills will be at par.

I suspect that Esau was a very busy man. I would be inclined to think that the pleasures of life were his. Well, it appears as if dad got the son he had always wanted. Waiting twenty years made the taste sweeter. We need to remember that it takes two to dance in pairs. This is where Rebekah comes in.

When the time of delivery was over, I suppose that both of the children were placed into the hands of the mother. I am sure that dad said: "The red one was the firstborn. The other one came right behind hanging onto the heels of the red one."

The twins were evidently not identical. Mom probably looked at the other one (Jacob) and thought, he really is a lot cuter than the red one. I think that Jacob put a sparkle in the eyes of Rebekah right from the outset.

It might have been that when she looked in at night, she always checked Jacob's cradle first, to see if everything was all right.

My feeling is that Jacob must have stuck close by mom as he was growing up. If mom went to draw water at the well, Jacob tagged along. When she went to prepare dinner, he probably peeled the potatoes. Maybe he had a snack as he helped Rebekah cut the roast. Jacob was content to hang around. He did not always have to be out doing something to be happy.

The Bible does say, "Godliness with contentment is great gain." It is a good thing that Jacob was like this. Had he not been, he may have been violent when he went in search of his bride. Dear old uncle Laban was a bit crooked in his dealings with Jacob at this time, and this would affect Jacob.

When I consider the matter of crooked dealings, my attention is drawn to Rebekah and Jacob. Nevertheless, before I can pass on this picture from the Bible for your evaluation, I would like to present a short movie for your viewing pleasure. The story line comes from a movie that I viewed some time ago: "A Big Hand, For a Little Lady."

Please follow me back to the pioneer days, when men wore their gun belts at their side. It was a time when they overran main street saloons with gambling, and other unacceptable practices. These places also happened to be the places where someone could find lodging, as they travelled from town to town.

We can well imagine that the saloon would not be the best place for a family to come and live. The noise would be enough to keep anyone on the edge, especially if they were trying to get the young ones to bed.

As I focus on this scene, I see a young couple and their son riding into town. For the sake of interest, I will call the name of this town Futureville. Try to picture this couple with all their earthly possessions loaded on this horse drawn wagon. I can see excitement in their eyes as they approach the edge of town. People are casually going about their affairs. I see dogs roaming the streets, and horses hurriedly coming and going. The place seems a buzz with activity.

Well it has been a long haul from Southern California to Futureville. The trail has been hot and dusty as they travelled the distance. The thought of a clean place to stay, and a place to wash up is an inviting thought.

For the sake of reference, I will call these folks, Jesse, Jane, and Johnny. Try to visualize them as they approach the saloon. They step down off their wagon and venture up onto the boardwalk in front of the saloon. I can see a look of trepidation, and one of anticipation: After all, they left everything back home to make a new life here.

So far the town may be more vibrant than they had expected. They had pictured Futureville as a peaceful place: A place where they could raise a family and feel the freshness of God's green earth.

Silence invades this hive of illicit activity, as this family of three enters the saloon. All eyes suddenly focus on an unusual sight. Here they stand, Jesse, Jane, and little Johnny. They were as ridged as if displayed in a showcase. If there is such a thing as a homey family type look, it was smeared all over this family.

People like this did not usually set a foot in a place of this nature. The saloon had its share of dancing girls, booze, and gambling. Why in the world did Jesse choose this place to lodge his family, till he could find better accommodations? So, the question is: Who does a person see about getting a room in this place? Cautiously, and hand in hand they approach the bar.

Finally Jane breaks the silence as she asks about lodging. In a show of disbelief, big Jake the bar tender asks if they are sure they have the right place. As she looks upwards toward the second level, Jane assures big Jake that they do need a room for a few days.

As if in a hurry to keep these unlikely occupants from the contamination of their surrounding, big Jake shows them to their room. During the preliminaries, Jesse has noticed that something is going on in the back room. Just as he is making inquiry about what is taking place in the back room, a dignified looking gentleman approaches the bar. While this man is making his request for more poker chips, Jesse realizes what is going on.

When Jessie realizes what is happening, his heart begins to thump uncontrollably. It was as if a hundred thousand pairs of horse's hooves were stomping over every molecule of his anatomy. Poker had almost been the ruination of their lives in the past. For the most part, this had been the reason for leaving their last hometown. Jesse asked if he could watch.

Jesse was still in the stage of having withdrawal pains. He only wanted to watch these men play the game. He thought that everything would be all right if he could only watch. This would ease the pains of withdrawal for him. His wife was very insistent that he should not even watch the game. Still, Jesse insisted that he only wanted to watch.

After some diligent thought, the dignified gentleman finally consents to allowing Jessie to watch. Jane finally said that if he were to go into the room to observe the proceedings, he would have to take their son in there with him. With a great deal of disgust from the other gamblers, Jesse and Johnny went in and watched this annual affair.

The men, who were regulars, in this yearly game of poker, were wealthy men. Each of them dropped everything they were doing when it came time to take part in this big extravaganza.

One of these gamblers left in the middle of his daughters wedding. Others also left important matters of business to be involved in this affair.

This was no small matter. This was a day of serious card playing. It was a precarious situation. An intense atmosphere filled the room into which Jesse placed himself and his son.

After some time of just watching the others play, Jesse figured that he would have a chance to increase the little pile of cash that he and Jane had managed to put aside: To start fresh in this new town. After some disputing between the gamblers, they gave Jesse the opportunity to get into the game. His wife had no knowledge of what was happening.

Over a period of some playing time, Jessie lost a considerable amount of the money they had saved to come to their new home. Finally when nearly all hope, and nearly all the money was gone, Jesse got what he considered a winning hand. The problem was that he ran out of money in the middle of the biggest pot he had ever seen. This presented a serious problem. He did not have much choice but to throw in his hand.

As he endeavoured to figure out a way to get enough money to finish the hand, he had a heart attack. They summoned his wife, and there was a time of heartbreak as she thought about the two problems she faced. One was the state of health of her husband, while the other was the matter of being in this strange town and losing everything they had.

Jessie had enough strength left within him, to give Jane the cards. He asked her to finish the game. One huge obstacle remained: She did not have any money left.

During some negotiating with the other gamblers, she tried to sell their team of horses and their wagon. None of the other gamblers would likely give her enough of a purse to finish the game. Each man felt he had the winning hand.

While all this haggling was in process, Jane decided to go to the bank for a loan, using Jessie's cards as collateral. It was a tough task to convince the bank manager to give her a loan, using something as unprofessional as a poker hand. However, she succeeded.

Well, the bank manager came along to help her play out the hand. Everything turned out well for the little lady with the big hand. She won a large bundle of money. The poker game broke up, and all the men went back to their separate homes. Apparently justice was served, or was it?

At the end of the movie, we saw a strange assortment of personnel. The doctor got involved because of the heart attack had by Jesse. Another person at the table was the banker. Then there was the homey little family. Everybody sat around a table full of money. Little Johnny evenly distributed shares among all of them. Jane and Jesse were not actually husband and wife. The deception had been planned, and successfully orchestrated.

Now, while this movie is fresh in our minds, let's think back to the time when I discussed the birth of the twins. Remember that I said that I thought Isaac and Rebekah both believed the forecast, of what God said would happen in the lives of the boys.

In view of that knowledge I thought it was an act of great faith that they named the second boy Jacob. Tradition would have to be broken, if it were going to happen the way that God had predicted.

I find myself of the opinion that only one parent remembered for very long, the words spoken by God. According to my rationalization, this is where all the future problems in this family began.

If we have read the story of this family affair, we should notice that Isaac soon began to think of Esau as the next titleholder to the family farm. Isaac may have overlooked the word of God spoken earlier, but Rebekah had not.

Icicles would be hanging from the overhanging rooftop of her house on a day in July, before Rebekah would let anything stand between Jacob and the winner's purse. This was a very determined lady. She had a memory equalled by none. I also believe that she may have clued Jacob in on what God had said: At the beginning.

Rebekah remembered the time when Esau gave away the birth right to Jacob during a fit of hunger. She probably thought to herself: "That was step one." That part happened to take place without any scheming taking place. Now that Isaac was dropping hints that he would soon pass on the blessing, step two is about to happen. Rebekah had plenty of time to plan for this occasion.

The big scam described a picture of what happened in the lives of Becky and Ike. To me it was a portrayal of the story of Esau and Jacob. When I saw the movie, everything looked natural and above board for some time.

During the early stages, I thought everything was not going to be like a Sunday afternoon picnic, for the delightful little family. I thought there would be a bear or two in the park, to spoil this pleasurable little family outing. It was not until near the end of the movie that I saw the devious plot that they had perpetrated to defraud someone of their possessions. It worked. The bears in the park were left without their lunch.

As I begin to cover the factual story of this Biblical family of Isaac, Rebekah, Esau and Jacob. It is my intention for us to remember some innocent scenes of their entry: As we go on to the point where they put the last nail into the coffin.

For Isaac, I believe that it was as though they finally put him into his coffin prematurely. The onslaught against his disabled, unrecoverable condition, affected him. People really feel this kind of pain, when someone cons them beyond reason. Please stay with me as we go on to the fight of the century. ·

Get your tickets for:
The Big Prize Fight!

The Big Prize Fight!

And Jacob sod pottage: and Esau came from the field, and he was faint: And Esau said to Jacob, Feed me, I pray thee, with that same red pottage; for I am faint: therefore was his name called Edom. And Jacob said, Sell me this day thy birthright. And Esau said, Behold, I am at the point to die: and what profit shall this birthright do to me?

And Jacob said, Swear to me this day; and he sware unto him: and he sold his birthright unto Jacob. Then Jacob gave Esau bread and pottage of lentiles; and he did eat and drink, and rose up, and went his way: thus Esau despised his birthright. Genesis 25:29-34

Chapter 7

Somehow, when I survey the scenes depicted in the story of Isaac and Rebekah, I see them as two managers in the sport of boxing. One on the side of the fighter expected to win: While the other one is in the process of grooming the underdog, but they do not seem to realize that to be the situation.

Earlier, in this section of the book, I laid out some ways that may have caused this turn of events. Rather than it turning out to be two fighters on the same team fighting for the crown, which they would share, (like an Olympic team): We are presented with two fighters, and managers who are fighting against each other in the title bout.

This split began to take place when one parent, who initially shared the same word spoken by God, forgot some lines while he played his part. This seemingly small error would turn out to be one with serious consequences. In some ways there would be no winner.

In every fight of major proportion: Such as Muhammad Ali vs. George Foreman, the purse for the fight is also of major proportion. The money, which they receive from ticket sales and other revenues, is enough to cover the winners and the loser's share of the purse: and the other expenses. A huge difference exists between the amounts that the winner receives, in relationship to the loser's portion.

When we look at the fight between Esau and Jacob, apparently Jacob won, and he did. Still, the cost of this victory, far exceeded the revenues that Jacob gleaned from the fight proceeds. Noticing this fact is not hard, as we look at the big picture.

Some of costs incurred were related to family rifts, which may never have healed. Two nations would evolve from one family. They would never be unified. For all the time that men are left to their own devices on this earth, a constant battle will exist between them.

If we look at the conflicts that Israel has faced because of this family feud, and count all the costs, and compare them with the gains, I believe that we would come up with a tremendous deficit.

Is there any way in which one can measure the cost of a struggle for control between a husband and a wife? A blending of purpose never comes through this kind of relationship: It is like the old tug of war game we played as kids. One rope, and a gang of kids on each end, this was all that we needed: Each group trying to drag the other ones down to the ground.

I wonder if they ever settled the struggle between Isaac and Rebekah before death parted them: If not, then the cost for the victory was not worth the victor's purse. Many tasks have to be performed during the preparations for a prizefight.

Arrangements must be made for the sight for the fight. Advertising and promotions need some attention. All of these items are categorized al under administrative duties.

Both managers have many preliminary duties to perform. Each of them must set up the best possible training facilities for their fighters. The manager also needs to scout the camp of the opposing fighter, to find out some weaknesses that are apart of his make-up. The manager has many matters to consider in preparation for the title bout.

Not everything is done for the fighters. The combatants have a responsibility to fulfill some preliminary preparations for themselves. They have to be trust worthy enough to follow all the rules outlined by those in authority over them. Every infraction incurred, can give their opponent an advantage over them, and cause possible victory to be certain defeat. Winning is the only thing that is important in a title fight. Second best is not good enough.

I have decided to use the analogy of the fight game, because I see a tremendous amount of in fighting in this patriarchal family. Family feuding was an integral part of the lives of Isaac's predecessors. It seemed to carry on as Esau and Jacob struggled to leave the womb of their mother. While looking at this picture, I see Jacob fighting so that he would not be left behind: Because he was hanging onto the heels of Esau.

In any match up of boxers, we will always find a favourite. It may be because one combatant has more fight experience than the other: Or, one of them may have a better knock out punch. It is up to the promotion's department to put the fighters on display. I see the billboard displayed like this:

Family Feud
ESAU vs. JACOB

The winner's share of the purse is, "To be the chief of the family, for the Jewish race." The loser may as well be dead, because, when we consider his future; it is non-existent. The managers for the combatants are:

ISAAC & REBEKAH.
The trainers for both fighters are,

Life Itself. The sight for the title bout is: Somewhere Along Life's Road.

I would say that during the early years Jacob and Esau were only brothers because they had the same mother and father. When I think about their physical appearance, I find them to be considerably separated. Esau was of a reddish complexion, while Jacob was more of a fairer complexion. Each of their natures was also contrary to the other.

As they grew up, brotherly love is not the strong characteristic that they share. I see them as competitors all the way along their journey. I feel that Esau was not much concerned with the conditioning required to be the heavyweight champ. I think he may have been mean enough to win the battle of the mind, but he lacked the sufficient skills to out manoeuvre his opponent.

Esau was self-indulgent concerning the pleasures of life. He was a real man. He was a hunter. I understand him to be one with a gruff voice. I think he was all brawn, and little brain. Esau was careless about the serious concerns of life. Esau seemed to need the tangible entities of life. A good steak right now more effectively replaces the promise of a blessing down the road.

Esau never took the wishes of his parents seriously. They did not want him to intermarry with the Canaanites, but he did so anyhow. He also may have been a spiteful man. I have yet to see anything that gives me the impression that Esau trained seriously: For what should have been his most valued possession.

65

He was supposed to take the leadership role after his father died. Leadership carries along with it a heavy responsibility to serve others before oneself. Esau did not seem to have the capabilities, to take on that role.

What was it that made Esau the number one contender? When we survey the characteristics of this man, they do not appear to make him a good candidate. As I see it, the only thing that made him the odds on favourite, was that he was born first. That is it! He had been in the fight game just a little bit longer than Jacob. Esau had won the first match. Out of a set of twins, he came first.

With skills such as displayed by this brawler, the only fights he would ever win, would be those in which his opponent had no wit. If his opponents were weaker mentally and physically, then he could be guaranteed championship.

When a promoter is pushing a boxing match he is concerned about many more aspects than just the physical stature of a man. He will base his predictions on a thorough evaluation of everything it takes to be a winner. I feel that we have taken a very good Photostat of the number one contender for the heavyweight crown. Isaac would vacate the crown. The old champ was getting a bit too old. He had held the title for many years. It was time to find a successor.]'

Along with Esau, another young man was eligible to contend for the vacated crown. His name is Jacob. Jacob does not have the appearance of being a heavyweight, but we need to take a closer look at this candidate.

Right from the time he was born, Jacob gave me the impression that he would go to any lengths to be number one. I saw it in the delivery room when he was hanging onto Esau's heels for dear life: as he emerged from the womb.

This may seem inconsequential to some, but not to me. We often use first impression in the naming of a child. Similarly, using distinguishing signs of the actual birth to discern a part of someone's character is possible. Esau came out rough and ready looking, and he turned out to be an outdoorsman. He had time only for the segments of life that would take care of his insatiable desire for immediate self-gratification.

Jacob came out fair looking, and reaching out for life with intensity. Jacob was a homebody. I see this as someone who stayed at home. This gave him time to sort out the important matters in life, before they snuck up on him like a lion would stalk his prey. Jacob had a chance to look at the big picture and say: "I am going to be a part of it in a big way."

The more I study the birth of Jacob and Esau, the more I see how even all the minor details were not minor at all. Every detail pointed to the outcome for both of them. I am not insinuating that being an outdoorsman is wrong. Nor am I suggesting that the rest of what Esau was, made him unfit. Yet, Esau did not have a proper balance in life. He was unfit for the challenge of winning the title match.

One of our sons is an avid fisherman. He also has a job and a wife, and children; he knows and respects those commitments. Nobody can convince me that he would not spend all his time fishing, if he did not have these positions to honour. I may very well be right behind him if I were in that position.

One morning I phoned him to relay to him the fact that they cancelled our job for the day. It was an exceptionally cold day at the end of December. I said to him: "I suppose you are not too disappointed." He replied by saying": I was prepared for whichever way it went."

I had told him the night before that there was a possibility of this happening. So he might have gotten his hopes up to go ice fishing. But in his reply, I could see that he didn't have the Esau syndrome. Let's look at what God thought about these two men.

"Was not Esau Jacob's brother?"

Yet I have loved Jacob, but Esau I have hated, and have turned his mountains into a wasteland and left his inheritance to the desert jackals. Malachi 1:2&3

God saw that Esau did not have a concern about his birthright, until he was about to lose it. Then suddenly his right of birth also became apart of self, and now. God is serious about the things He gives us. We need to be as well.

I am not sure that I could become a birth analyst. I don't think that I could look at any newborn and begin to set out the path they would take. Still, sometimes in retrospect I can put together this kind of picture for character analysis.

I think Jacob was ready to start putting the pieces together for his ultimate title match. Yes, the parents had a definite part to play in the way in which the lads would mature. Nevertheless, an inherent nature would supersede what the parents would impart to the children.

One skirmish which Esau and Jacob faced, took place after Esau had been out on the hunt for some time. When he returned he was half dead with hunger. This is when he saw Jacob mastering the art of cooking. Jacob was making a savoury stew.

Immediately he approached him and began to beg for something to eat. At this point Jacob saw an opportunity to exploit a weakness in his opponent.

It was not long before he took note of this first flaw in the number one contender. Jacob said, "If you give me your right of position as the first born, then you can help yourself to some stew, buddy." Esau could not see past his zest for self-gratification: So he gave him his oath. Jacob had just acquired the right to the major part the inheritance. Look at it closely. The knock out punch was struck long before the title bout took place.

Jacob had just paid a visit to the enemy camp to pick up on any advantage he could gain. A great deal of strategy was involved in this manoeuvre. Flick back with me to the last chapter and reflect along with me, how people were caught off guard. (An example of this is in the story of Jessie, Jane and family.)

It is easy to see the reason why this planned deception succeeded. People, who were usually firm in their decision, began to allow things that caught them off guard. If we look back at the poker game, we will remember that it had previously always been a closed affair: Now they left themselves open for damage because they allowed for a stranger to come in.

In any scenario of the deceived and the deceiver, we have those who have their eyes and ears open. We also have those who are caught completely of f guard. It is here that we can align the fighters and the managers into two columns:

Deceivers' & Deceived - Winner's & Losers.

I have related how Jacob was watchful and ready all along the way. In Rebekah I have seen eagerness, and a readiness to fight. These two are not be in the column of the deceived in this instance. In Esau's case, noticing his disregard for life is not very hard. He had a distinct carelessness about life. He was plainly vulnerable to deception.

Isaac was a good man, but he closed his eyes long before he literally became blind. Isaac became vulnerable to deception when he did this. He had disregarded what God had said before the birth of his sons: "The older shall serve the younger."

Often we hear about groups of people whom they have conned out of their savings. This becomes a possibility, when we are not fully aware of all the facts. Typically, it happens because people think that they really are going to get the deal of a lifetime. Often, when they cut the price, they cut the product. It is like the heroin dealer who cuts the dope: He does this so that he can make a greater profit.

Isaac should never have gotten to the point where he expected to pass on the blessing to Esau. He let himself think that God had spoken, but had forgotten what God had said at the beginning.

Any deviation from the schedule can cause one to falter when they get into the ring. By the time we get to the ringside, it is much too late to make the move to condition our self.

To get the clearest possible picture, we need to read the actual account of this story in the Bible. We can find this portion in Genesis 27. Take the time to reflect on the past, and consider the reason, that this time in the lives of these people, got so far out of context.

In Genesis 27, fight time has arrived. This fight was sold out a long time ago. Now, all we can do is watch. Round by round I watch, as they exchange blows. Between rounds the managers encourage the fighters to stick to the game plan, and to remember to do the things they had learned during training.

Watch, as Isaac unveils the fight plan for Esau's first punch in verse three: "Take your weapons and go out to the field and get some venison, so that I can place the winner's crown on your head." Then take careful note of Rebekah, as she sets up a counter punch in verse five: "Rebekah heard when Isaac spake to Esau." She had learned to keep her eyes and ears open over the training period. Watch closely as she manoeuvres her fighters' gloves to strike the punch. Observe it in verse nine? "Go now to the flock, and fetch me thence two good kids of the goats…"

Let me make some comparisons here, in the play-by-play commentary. Esau went to the field to ready himself. He did not have the necessary items to make the meal for his dad. Here, Esau did not have his gloves ready for the knock out punch.

Jacob on the other hand, went out to the flock that was close to where he was. He knew he had the necessary reserve, to throw a crushing blow. While Esau is running around the ring trying to land a hurting blow, Jacob is landing the punches.

If we have our eyes focussed on this fight, it will not take us long to see the strategy of Rebekah and Jacob. Just keep landing the punches, while Esau is on the ropes. I see Isaac in a bit of a daze, as he thinks aloud: "Where did he learn to fight like that?"

In reply to this question that was not directed at him, I hear Jacob saying: "I have been keeping my eyes and ears open Father. I have been preparing for this fight for a long time."

Isaac is confused with the swiftness of the array of punches thrown (Gen.27: 20) It is as though he is looking at one man in the ring, because what he is seeing, is not what he had put in the fight plan.

Suddenly, the bell rings. One fighter has hit the canvas. It is Esau: He is lying there on the raw canvas, cold as ice. The referee administers the final eight-count, and then he raises the hand of a fighter who is on his feet, and says:

The winner, by knock out: Jacob.

Follow the losing team to their dressing room and I listen to Isaac asking Esau: "What went wrong? What happened to the training exercises we talked about?"

Esau's reply goes something like this, "Well I guess I should have focussed more on the fight than I did; I had some pleasures that I wanted to enjoy, so I cheated on my training time a little."

"But dad, why didn't you watch me to see if I needed some pointers to help me along?"

"Well I guess I thought everything was under control, son."

With tears in his eyes, I can hear Esau choking, as he spoke these words, "I thought I had it won, I really did."

This was Esau's analogy of the proceedings of his life span to this point. For him there was still a considerable time left to turn life around. He was still in position to be able to win a few matches in life. For Isaac it was a different story.

This title bout for him and his fighter was the last.

The sight for this fight was:
Somewhere Along Life's Road!

Isaac was at the point where he had to give up his share of the crown. It was time for a successor to be found. While the losers are crying, and trying to sort out what should have been a clear-cut victory, the winners are celebrating. Manager and fighter are dancing the victory dance. Stay in your seats. Watch as we crown the winner.

The Winner's Crown is just ahead.

Jacob Bergen

The Winners Crown!

I have fought a good fight, I have finished my course, and I have kept the faith: Henceforth there is laid up for me a crown of righteousness, which the Lord, the righteous judge, shall give me at that day: and not to me only, but unto all them also that love his appearing. 2 Timothy 4:7&8

Chapter 8

Losing leaves us with nothing, but a bitter taste in our mouth. A loser usually always looks back and thinks: "I should have won." The loser often thinks that they unfairly treated him or her.

I have heard people say that victory is sweet. We have all watched as a sports team realizes their win. Here we have seen the picture of people raising their arms in the celebration. I can see myself saying, "All right! This is great!"

Our expressions of victory can come in all kinds of ways, but the overriding emphasis is, we see ourselves at the top. How sweet it is. The euphoria of it all will last for a time. Sometimes we ride on this high for longer than we should. I think that when this happens we leave ourselves open for a fall. When this happens it is because we are no longer focussed on the goal. All we want to do now is to carry the trophy around with us, and put ourselves in the spotlight.

Winning carries with it responsibility, for instance, the winner of a beauty pageant: Once they have crowned them, they have an agenda to follow. They travel around the country to represent the good will of their own country. They become involved in many different endeavours, because they have earned the right to be where they are.

In time it usually becomes necessary for the titleholder to defend their title. No matter what that title represents, someone somewhere, will eventually be there to try to dethrone them. Guarding against this danger is imperative. We need to keep in shape, or someday we will find the crying towel in our own hands. Yes, victory is sweet: We should not let it give us a tummy ache.

Many a young athlete has won acclaim for the skills they possessed. This isn't the problem. The trouble comes when they are unable to handle the pressure that comes with the territory. Sometimes people don't know when to put the crown on the shelf, and get on with the rest of their lives.

When I look at Jacob, I try to fit myself into the inner most part of the man. If I can do that, then I am better able to understand what he went through. This is easy to handle when I am in the euphoric stage of the victory: Here I can raise my arms to the sky and shout: I won! I won! I won!

73

As I sit in the place of Jacob, and the shine wears off the victory crown, the moments in the highlight, go from: I won! I won! I won! I won! I won? I won?

The way I see it, Jacob probably soon began to wonder if he had won the family farm or not. When things began to turn sour, Jacob must have begun to come back to reality. The reality of it was that Jacob had taken advantage of Esau's weakness. When someone takes advantage of us, it is no picnic. Esau was evidently not ready to turn the other cheek and let brotherly love prevail.

Esau was going to wait till dad passed away, and then it was his intention to get even with his brother. These kinds of feelings are really not that hard to understand. If there has never been a unified family, where the love relationship has had a chance to blossom, then contempt comes easily.

If I were to take the package presented in Gen. 27, and bring it into January 1/1993, I would have to wonder: "How, would I react if my name were Esau, and not Jacob?" When there is a considerable amount of prize money up for grabs, there is also a considerable amount of intensity involved. If there is nothing at stake, it is easier to say: "I'm a Christian, I would accept the consequence, whichever way it went."

Let's face it; it is easier talked than walked. Though Esau had been at fault in his respect for life, Jacob and his mom did him a dirty deed. This was going to be hanging over the head of Jacob for some time to come.

As we look at this picture of the family feud, seeing that there was a substantial amount of immediate cost is easy. This deduction is taken right off the top of the winner's share of the purse. The cost factor I am speaking about wasn't transacted with the monetary system of the day. It was much more than that. The wreckage of peoples' peace of mind was at risk here. It was going to mean gut wrenching heartache for family members.

For a person who is independently wealthy, paying a million-dollar ransom is easier than it is to lose a family member. For the person who has everything, paying a huge fine is easier, than it is to suffer penalties that involve the physical body. If we follow the fight game, we will notice some things that take place: one transaction is that revolving around the winner receiving his money.

They slice a big chunk of the purse off before the champ gets some cash. It's called taxes. As hard as it is to give up this portion of a big purse, it still leaves a great deal for the one who wears the winner's crown.

As I have followed the life of Jacob, I have come to take note that he kept on paying. It was not just a matter of paying the taxes, and then painting the town red: No, not a chance. Jacob was going to come up empty for a considerable time slot.

I wonder what Jacob would have done if he had looked ahead, during training for the big fight? While life was teaching him how to get ahead, he didn't seem able to add up the figures involved in reaching out for the title deed to: The Family Farm.

Some of Jacob's problems would have immediate consequences, while others would have long-term effects. Now is the time to look at some of his expenditures and see how the books balanced.

In receiving the prize (the blessing, or the right of the first born), Jacob was in charging expenses that we will see deducted from his purse. I see the initial expenses as of a threefold nature. Look at them with me briefly.

First, Jacob incurred the wrath of his father, who it seems had failed to instil in his son, the courtesy of fair play. So, the boy and his mother executed one of the biggest scams of all time.

When we look at this story, we can find enough of a reason to anger any man. It hurts immeasurably when someone is involved in ruining a personal relationship with another person. This is especially true when it is a relationship with those closest family members. Parents are probably the closest family members to whom we could relate. They were the first ones involved in our physical well-being. So, when we take part in ruining that human bond, the pain runs deep.

Secondly, Jacob puts himself into the position of not being able to have the explicit trust of his father. Trust is something that is a big plus for a young man when he is about to venture out on his own. I could be wrong, but I get the feeling that a degree of uncertainty resided in Isaac's mind: When he sent Jacob to find a wife. In Genesis 28, it states that Isaac blessed Jacob. Then it says that he charged (commanded) him not to pick a wife from the wrong race of people.

Esau had been guilty of this infraction. Yet, his father had been ready to entrust him with the leadership of the children of Israel. With Jacob,

Isaac felt that he needed to give a strong warning to Jacob, about not taking a wife from the daughters of Canaan. I can visualize Jacob thinking some tough thoughts. "Dad, why in your mind, was it right to pass on the blessing to Esau, though he married those Hittite women. You are reluctant to give it to me without warning me against the same thing that Esau did."

This reminds me of the times when our teens used to say, *"Don't you trust me?"* At times my reply has been, *"Of course we trust you. But???"* In our heart we were saying, "You're darn right we don't trust you."

Did this conversation ever occur with one of your children? I think that anyone, who has ever raised a family of any size, may have had conversations of this nature.

I really believe that God would have engineered the right ending to the story, without the help of the boy and his mom. The mistakes orchestrated here provide a tremendous opportunity for an education. Though there was a great deal of wrong doing in the whole scenario. In Romans 8:28; we read this: "...all things work together for good to them that love God, to them who are the called according to His purpose."

Thirdly, I see an expense that brings a great deal of sadness to my heart. This is the matter concerning Isaac and Rebekah, and what affect this whole issue had on their relationship with each other. Jacob had to chalk this up as part of the awful cost of victory.

Jacob had been a party to allowing disunity to grow between his mom and dad. However, I will not say that it was all Jacob's fault. Still, if he had said no to his mother, and said instead: "Mother, God will look after it." Then Jacob could have been a part of the positive, rather than the negative. He would have been a positive factor in the building of a relationship.

These three issues alone will be compounded often in the time span of Jacob's tenure on earth. Stay with me please as we add to the winner's charge account.

If we observed the winner of a boxing match at the victory party, we would expect to see a person who is ready to conquer the world.

When I look at Jacob, I see a man who is about to run from the loser. Looks to me as if this were supposed to be a fixed fight: This type of scenario is one we might expect to see in a gangster film. Esau was slated to be the winner, and now Jacob strikes the winning blow when he was supposed to take a fall. Because of his supposed wrongdoing, his life is threatened.

The fight did not go as planned by the fighter and his manager. After his brother threatens Jacob's life, Rebekah orchestrates another plan: One that will save the life of her son. She decides to keep some facts from Isaac; I suppose it was so that he would not need to face any more pain than that they had already confronted him with.

Rather than tell Isaac of the death threat, she thought that informing Isaac that it was time for Jacob to get married would be wise. To make sure that Jacob chose the right woman, they suggested that he go to Rebekah's home in Haran: Then the boy would take a proper wife. It does not matter how they cut the pie. They sent Jacob to flee for his life.

Remember, when it was time for Isaac to marry: Abraham sent someone to find a wife for his son. I believe that this would likely have happened here as well, if treachery had not altered the course of everyone's lives. When we look at how it all turned out, it allows for cause to wonder if Abraham's servant made a good choice for Isaac.

Many events took place because of Jacob's banishment to Haran. We could surmise that this was an event on which Jacob had not figured. I would have thought, that Jacob might have been of the mindset that he should stick around and learn from his dad. If he were to take over the leadership of a nation, a time of tutoring would have been appropriate, so that he could be more effective.

As time goes on, we will get a better picture of the actual training that took place in the life of Jacob. In fact, most of Jacob's training will come through the school of: "It's tough when you're out on your own." The costs that I am discussing are part of that training.

Jacob's departure would have far greater consequences than either he or his mother had anticipated. Rebekah thought of this trip as one of short duration. By sending Jacob away for a time, Rebekah is not deprived of both of her sons. I believe that she was already deprived of her son Esau, because of her part in the theft of his inheritance. I form this line of reasoning by reading Gen. 27.

And Esau hated Jacob because of the blessing wherewith his father blessed him: and Esau said in his heart, The days of mourning for my father are at hand; then will I slay my brother Jacob. And these words of Esau her elder son were told to Rebekah: and she sent and called Jacob her younger son, and said unto him, Behold, thy brother Esau, as touching thee, doth comfort himself, purposing to kill thee.

Now therefore, my son, obey my voice; and arise, flee thou to Laban my brother to Haran; And tarry with him a few days, until thy brother's fury turn away; Until thy brother's anger turn away from thee, and he forget that which thou hast done to him: then I will send, and fetch thee from thence: why should I be deprived also of you both in one day?

By looking carefully at Gen. 27:44, I am convinced that Jacob was only supposed to be gone for a limited amount of time. Scripture doesn't show us anything that would lead us to believe that Jacob and his mother ever crossed paths again. Historical writers also believe that when Jacob left, it was the last time Rebekah saw him.

I am beginning to wonder if there was anything left of the winner's share of the prize money. To this point, it looks to me like a large deficit has been created.

The trip Jacob was embarking on was not a vacation. He was not planning it just so that he could get rest and relaxation, because of the pressures the title bout had created. I for one am convinced that Jacob never really wanted to take this leave of absence.

I have a scriptural basis for my opinion of this scenario of events. It's found in Genesis 28:20&21. Please hear my paraphrased version of this text.

"God if you will give me a place to live, and if you will make sure that I don't starve to death…and more than anything else God, if you will make sure that I will get back home safely as soon as possible, then I will serve you, just like my father and grandfather did."

In my evaluation of this account in history, I feel that Esau would have been much better suited to go on this excursion. He was used to wandering about half crazed with hunger, never knowing where he would sleep tonight. Anywhere under he stars would be fine for him.

Jacob strikes me as more of a homebody. Isaac was like that too. He was not one to travel around as much as his father Abraham did. Isaac was more inclined to make sure he had enough water around the place. He was always digging wells.

His concerns were centred more around home.

Maybe this is why Isaac was only kind of, "The man in the middle." Much more detail is given about both his father, and his son. I see him as more of a u-joint: As in the drive train of a vehicle. I see him as the man who was supposed make sure that a connection would be made between Abraham, and Jacob.

Included in the list of expenses, which I would deduct off the royalties associated with wearing the winner's crown, I would insert the cost of Jacob's moving expenses.

There are only a few entities that I will allude to here, in the closing words of this part of the book. Jacob was yet to meet uncle Laban. This experience was going to prove to be an experience better done without.

The process of getting married to the girl of his dreams was not going to be as easy as it should have been. It was going to cost him 20 years. For the major portion, Jacob would be faced with the intimidation tactics of his uncle.

Added to these mere ulcer-creating goodies, was the fear that he would yet have to deal with when it came time for him to go home and face his brother. He wouldn't know till then, if the death threat were still on, or not. This matter would only be determined when he actually faced Esau.

There is a saying that, "Time heals all wounds." Maybe this should be worded to read: "Time sometimes heals all wounds." There have been many people, who when their time is up, have gone to the grave with a killing hatred in their hearts. I do not believe that there was any guarantee that everything was going to be rosy in the eyes of Esau, concerning his brother Jacob, at their next encounter.

In my sometimes-allegorical account of the life of Jacob, I have dealt with issues like: Jacob before his birth, Jacob, the boy, and some of Jacob the man. Whenever I have had occasion to think about this man, the overwhelming trait that comes to mind is, Jacob the Deceiver.

There are many more pieces to this puzzle than that. Some of these are, Jacob the man continued, Jacob the boyfriend, the husband, the father, the businessman, the runaway, the child of God, the brother again, the servant, the father of nations, and many more that I have not thought of as yet. In the next section of the book I will endeavour to cover many of these pieces of, Jacob the Puzzle.

When I consider a man like Isaac, I believe that I could write a book that has to do with being a type of Jesus Christ. If I were to negate this entity, I wouldn't have an easy time writing about Isaac. I see him as a link in a chain, but on both ends of the chain I see the driving forces: Things like a giant metal ball on each end, come to mind.

When the subject of Jacob came to mind as book material, I thought to myself, "There are certainly enough facts available to cover many books." What I do in this book will not cover all that can be done with Jacob.

Jacob is a subject that really has to do with all of us, on a personal everyday level. In the closing section of this book, will we really feel like screaming out, or will we want to whisper: My Name Is Jacob. What did you say?

My Name Is Jacob. I can't hear you!

My Name Is Jacob!

As I take you into the next section of the book, I do not want to leave you with the feeling that there are no positive scenes in this man's future. In the scope of time and eternity, I think we will be able to look at him as an artist might do. When the artist places this work in a proper position for viewing, I believe that you would have to agree with me, that the story of Jacob is a masterpiece:

A Masterpiece of the work of God.

Part Three

Jacob The Puzzle

Jacob Bergen

Jacob The Man, And More.

Then Jacob went on his journey, and came into the land of the people of the east. And he looked, and behold a well in the field, and, lo, there *were* three flocks of sheep lying by it; for out of that well they watered the flocks: and a great stone *was* upon the well's mouth. And thither were all the flocks gathered: and they rolled the stone from the well's mouth, and watered the sheep, and put the stone again upon the well's mouth in his place. And Jacob said unto them, My brethren, whence *be* ye? And they said, Of Haran *are* we. And he said unto them, Know ye Laban the son of Nahor? And they said, We know *him*. And he said unto them, *Is* he well? And they said, *He is* well: and, behold, Rachel his daughter cometh with the sheep. Genesis 29:1-6

Jacob Bergen

Chapter 9

At the time that Jacob left his father and mother to go to uncle Laban's place, he was well into the experience of manhood. Until this point in his life, Jacob seemed to have reached an acceptable plateau. What might have begun as a childhood dream finally became a reality when he was guaranteed the role of patriarch of Israel.

His twin brother Esau had already married, but Jacob had remained single. I am not sure why he went so long without marrying. Maybe it was because he wanted to find out the will of his parents in the matter. The small matter of fulfilling his parent's wishes may not be a matter important to Esau. He married a couple of young women that were displeasing to his folks.

During this time of family conflict, Isaac and Rebekah sent Jacob to find himself a bride. Isaac had given Jacob clear instruction on the matter of whom not to marry.

This pending adventure was to begin a new era in this man's life. As a part of his manhood to this juncture, Jacob had been a manipulator. I see this as a trait that he might have inherited from his mother's side of the family. This will become more evident as we continue.

Jacob had scored big time, because of his deceptive tactics. He had won the fight by knockout. In the days ahead, the reverse will be the case for him. Jacob is embarking on a course that will see him go from being the deceiver, to the position of being the deceived.

We reap what we sow. If we only observed our own lives, and those of our families, I think this fact would be well illustrated. As I draw a portrait of this in my mind, I see that the last scene says, "If we do right things, right things are going to happen for us."

In womanhood, or manhood, each of us has to face both good times, and difficulties. These issues will prepare us for the future. Jacob had faced mostly good times, as far as looking out for number one. Nevertheless, the pendulum was beginning to swing the other way. As it was for Esau, Jacob may have failed in training properly for the next fight of his life.

Before these adverse circumstances would begin to haunt Jacob, he was going to experience his first romance: At least it is the first one that I can find recorded. He had packed his bags and set out in the direction of a place called Haran.

As I have searched the scriptures, I have observed that Jacob had a meeting with a V.I.P. before he got to Haran. Jacob met with his Maker. The meeting that I visualize is an extremely important event. It set the stage for the relationship Jacob, and God were going to have later.

As Jacob left his home, his greatest concern was that God would give him some sort of guarantee that he would get back home from this excursion. Then he could concentrate on the business of looking for the woman of his dreams.

During this executive meeting, both parties made commitments. The V.I.P. promised that He would prosper Jacob abundantly, and He would never leave him, no matter where he went.

Sometimes I wonder if we realize that we also have a commitment made to us, when we receive Jesus as our personal Savior. It is covered under a heading entitled, "The Earnest of the Spirit."

This issue can be studied in 2 Corinthians 1:22; 5:5, and Ephesians 1:14. I just took this slight detour, so that we would see that these people in the Bible were not any different from us. If we are looking for guarantees, then we ought to check out this one.

As I read the 28th. Chapter of Genesis, I see that it is God that makes the first move in the direction of making promises. Jacob was well on his way into the journey, when he got tired and did what comes naturally, he went to sleep. This is when God came to him in a dream.

When Jacob awoke out of his sleep, he understood something very plainly. He had stumbled into the presence of God, and he had not even noticed it. Nevertheless, once this became evident to him he began to do something about it. He had heard, and now he was about to send a communiqué to his Guarantor about his commitment to cement the relationship.

Jacob used his head here. First he picked up what he had (his pillow, not his promise), and he used it to build a church: Bethel was the name of it. Bethel is the place that he came to later, while working on his promise to God. Before we arrive at Haran, I would like for us to hear the words this traveler gave to the V.I.P.

"...If God will be with me and watch over me on this journey I am taking and will give me food to eat and clothes to wear so that I return safely to my father's house, then the Lord will be my God and this stone that I have set up as a pillar will be God's house, and of all that you give me I will give you a tenth." Gen.28: 20-22

Jacob left the church with faith in his heart. According to his own words he said, "...of all that He gives me..."

He had come into the presence of God. When he realized it, he acted upon it. He was encouraged enough to believe that he had a real meeting with God, and then he went on his way. When he arrived at his destination, he was going to be treated to some beautiful happenings.

Jacob had just been in contact with the most important being ever to exist. Apparently, he began by only seeing life through his own eyes, and not through the eyes of God. Jacob (Israel), the prince with God, had not yet been born. Because of this factor, he may have let outer beauty be his guide. Jacob should have been looking for the inner character of a woman as the drawing card to choose a wife.

When any one of us sees a person for the first time, we form an opinion about that person in the direction of favor, or in disfavor. This is especially true if one is in the market for a husband, or a wife. They can classify it as beauty, whether or not it is the kind exemplified in a Miss America Pageant, or the Mr. Universe contest.

We all know what it is that has to be displayed in some major proportions, to be a good candidate for first prize in one of these contests. Sometimes, distinguishing what causes a person to be attracted to someone else is hard for an outsider to imagine. I have often heard people say, " I cannot imagine what he sees in her, or I cannot imagine what she sees in him."

Think back for yourself, to the time when you began to form a love relationship with the person who is now your marriage partner. Was it only a physical attraction that caused your relationship to blossom into a lifetime commitment, or was it something more than that?

When I look at the picture presented in Gen.29, involving Jacob; the first thing that I see is that there was something in his heart concerning the matter of having found the right family. Then he saw the young woman, and her beauty. I have always thought that the first thing that Jacob ever noticed, or was concerned about, was the beauty of Rachel. Nevertheless, as I looked at this passage again, I began to take notice, that there were a few other matters, about which he was concerned.

First, I began to wonder if he had ever even seen these relatives before. It is after all, a considerable distance from Beersheba to Haran. Not only is it distant, but also according to the map, the terrain is hard to travel. People did not just hop into their van, fill up with gas, and head on out: As if it were a quick and easy trip.

If he had never laid eyes on these members of the clan, then there must have been a noticeable amount of excitement in his heart over this first meeting. After all, he had come here with an ulterior motive. He had not come just to say hello, and having finally met you folk is delightful. Jacob had come to marry someone from this tribe of people; he had come to take one of theirs.

Keep in mind; no matter what was brooding in the mind of this manipulator, the tradition of these folks was going to be kept in tact. We are going to become acutely aware of this when we finally get to the matrimonial trail.

The issue, that caused Jacob's problems, was that he was not going to have considered the fact that other people have their own way of doing things. It was up to him to respect that. Jacob had missed this little fact here, just like he did not realize that he had come into the presence of God at Bethel. It was a while before he figured out the rules of the game.

As I scan the account of this first encounter with Rebekah's family, I see that he has a willingness to serve: Especially after he laid eyes on Rachel. After he has displayed this willingness to serve her family, he is no longer able to contain himself. He starts to babble about anything that comes into his head. He begins to cry, and kisses Rachel.

Laban, "The Father of The Bride" to be, made an astute observation sometime during their initial times of fellowship. He told Jacob, "…You are my own flesh and blood."

Somewhere in this segment of the puzzle, I begin to visualize Laban saying: "You are just like us, my boy," and in light of this hypothetical fore thought, I see him as thinking to himself, "I wonder what is in it for me."

The story goes on to say that Jacob boarded there for a month. It seemed proper to Jacob to suggest, that if he were going to stick around and keep working around the place, that they should compensate him in some way.

I guess that somewhere during that first month, Jacob had begun to focus on the beauty of Rachel. The reason I can say this, is that Jacob has a reply for Laban, when they ask him what his wages are to be. His reply is, "Just Give Me Rachel!"

When someone really begins to love somebody, the price of the relationship is not really a factor. When Laban and Jacob began to discuss the terms of the marriage contract, the groom to be, inferred those seven years of service would be fair trade.

It was not as though Laban just made an offer, and said to him: "Work for me for seven years and then see if I can give Rachel to you." Laban signed the deal when he said, "...It is better that I give her to you than to some other man. Stay here with me."

When Jacob offered to work for Laban he specifically told him that he would make this deal for the younger daughter. There was not any confusion in the mind of this man about which young woman he loved.

Jacob was accustomed to making deals. He had done it when he stole his brother's blessing. He was also used to having to wait for the deals to appear. Until this point, he was not used to making an agreement and receiving his goods right away.

The situation, which we find Jacob in, is like when someone is buying a piece of property. In the details of the property value, one paragraph that states that there is oil in the ground. The oil is not just standing around in barrels waiting for somebody to cart it off to the refinery. There is going to be a considerable amount or cost and waiting, to attain the goods.

Jacob knew full well that there was value in the young woman, for whom he was offering to give up seven years of his life. I believe that he was acutely aware of Rachel's physical beauty. It may be something of which the men of Abraham's family were always cognitive.

Sarah, and Rebekah were both considered beautiful enough to cause their husbands to lose sleep over them: Especially, when other notable men, such as kings were in the area.

We have covered these stories earlier, so I will not digress here, to elaborate on them. I am sure that Jacob and Rachel spent a good deal of time together now that they contracted them to each other. It sounds kind of business like, when terms such as contracted to each other, are used. Here it was more than that. Jacob and Rachel loved each other. This gave them reason to spend seven years in joyful planning for that special day.

89

Scripture records the fact that it seemed as if it were only a short time for Jacob to wait. When he made the agreement with Rachel's father, he could already see it as in the present, not in the future. Jacob had a great love for this young lady, and because of this he can bridge the gaps that time would present.

During the final days of the completion of his contract with Laban, I can see Jacob's excitement level reaching a climax. It was like when he realized that be had finally come to the right place in his trek from Beersheba.

As we reach this V.I.D.. (Very Important Date) in his life, Jacob may not yet have realized the costs incurred: In his dealings to win the title deed to all he had attained. I have covered some of these costs, but that was more from my perspective than it may have been from Jacob's vantage point.

Until now, Jacob had only ever gotten everything that he wanted, except possibly the death threat from his brother. It is really not that hard to live life when everything is turning to gold right there on your plate. When Jacob woke up in the mornings, all he can smell was the rose bush. Stink weeds did not grow in his garden. I would say: That's living.

When a person is living the fast and easy life, apparently no other kind exists. We may not even be aware of others, who are not in the same deportment as ourselves. The focal point of ones' life is me, and mine.

Much of what I have seen in Jacob the man, and more, has been all cookies and ice cream. I think of the scenario of a person who goes to the most posh places in town to eat. They have no problem being catered to. If we do not like something, the management will gladly oblige your every whim. It is a little different at your local greasy spoon café. Here we could be faced with, "Listen buddy, if you don't like it, get out!"

More than just goodies exist in our lives. Part of being a real men or women, suggests that we are going to have to trek through the trenches from time to time. Jacob would soon become aware of some of these factors.

During the process of writing this chapter, I went to the funeral of a church family friend. It almost felt as though it might have been a real family member, although I know that I could not possibly feel the way they did. I just want to share something that one family member wrote as part of the eulogy.

The phrase which interested me the most, was when Don told us about the value he derived from the callouses, on his mom's feet. He used to rub them for her often. During these times he would share with her the incidents in his life that were dear to him. These conversations were of immeasurable value. When she was in the hospital during her final days, Don took occasion to rub her feet while she lay their suffering. He said:

"Now the callouses are gone, and so is the conversation."

The thing that I want to glean from this is, that if there have never been any hard times; there may never have been any precious moments. Jacob, the man, was yet to see what this man consisted of. The tough times lay ahead of him. I wonder to myself: If he had known what lay ahead, would he have stuck it out for seven years?

Stay with me please for:

Jacob the Boyfriend and Family Man.

Jacob The Boyfriend, And Family Man

Leah was tender eyed; but Rachel was beautiful and well favored. And Jacob loved Rachel and said; I will serve thee seven years for Rachel thy younger daughter. And Laban said, It is better that I give her to thee, than that I should give her to another man: abide with me. And Jacob served seven years for Rachel; and they seemed unto him but a few days, for the love he had to her. And Jacob said unto Laban, Give me my wife, for my days are fulfilled, that I may go in unto her. Genesis 29:17-21

Chapter 10

Have you ever involved yourself in the art of solving puzzles? I have often undertaken this task. Sometimes it is a task, not an art. When someone is in the market to find a puzzle, there is a wide range of puzzles from which to choose. I could show you crossword puzzles, puzzle where they join dots to form a picture, and a host of others. My favorite kind of puzzle is a picture puzzle.

As a youth, I spent many hours assembling these scenic works of art, along with my mom, and other family members. We would start doing the border, and then begin to work it out from there. At times, there would be a tangled mess of hands reaching here and there across the table, as each of us found a place for the piece in our hands. When the puzzle was nearly finished, I always tried to put the last piece in place: It seems as if the rest of the group was trying to do the same thing.

The life of Jacob is a giant puzzle. I would like to change many things in this puzzle. I ask the question: "Why did he go about to defraud his brother of the birthright? He knew that it was the right of the oldest in the family to receive it?" If it had been in my power to do something about the cruelty displayed in this part of his life, I would have done it.

Another part of the puzzle that I would have changed, in this picture of Jacob's life, is the way that Jacob was involved in deceiving his blind old dad. Certain times in the life of this man are hard to figure out. Why did he not have the insight to change certain situations himself? Take for instance, the time when he negotiated the deal to be married to Rachel. Jacob should have been aware of the customs of the folks from which he intended to retrieve a bride.

As I trudge through this book on the life of Jacob, I am increasingly amazed to see how God is intending to use Jacob: Though he has been a scheming operator. If I had the tools to have changed the blueprint of this puzzle, I would have rearranged it. I would make the picture show us that everyone's integrity is in tact.

God had the tools to do this, why didn't He rearrange the scenes to make it all come out better? I guess that I will accept the fact that God wanted certain pieces of the puzzle to go into prescribed areas. He wanted to show us that He could change anybody.

One scripture in the Bible says this: "Does not the potter have the right to make out of the same lump of clay some pottery for a noble purpose and some for common use?" Romans 9:21

As I look at what I have written to this point, I would say that I have begun to put together the pieces of the puzzle, which relate to bordering the main story. We have placed the pieces of this puzzle that relate to Jacob's ancestry, his birth, and his general upbringing.

In chapter nine I tried to begin the part where he goes out on his own. This is where I place him into the central part of the picture puzzle of life. I see him at the bottom edge of the puzzle (in a hypothetical sense of course). Jacob embarks onto a path that begins to wind uphill through a heavily forested area. Jacob starts to make the climb.

As he ventured out, he looked up beyond the maze of trees and saw a ray of sunlight. The view had a special affect on him. When he reached this special place, he was excited about what he saw. It was Rachel, and the knowledge that he had reached his destination.

Anyone who has ever put together a jigsaw puzzle involving trees, skies and water, will acknowledge that those are the hard parts to assemble. Putting together buildings large objects and people, are easier.

Usually, some sections of the border on a jigsaw puzzle include parts of the main theme. It's not all useless filler. The border helps us to find our way to the heart of the matter.

In this part of the puzzle, I will include the portions of Jacob's life until his departure to Haran. Now, in the heart of the scenes of life, Jacob the man is one frame of the whole scenario. He has begun to work with his hands in an attempt to prove his capabilities. He has shown himself to be strong.

When considering Jacob's strength, it was in two areas that he exhibited strength. He was physically strong, and he was manipulative. In matters concerning women Jacob was a pushover. Remember, that his mom was easily able to persuade him to join her in a deceptive cause.

When it came to looking for a wife, he fell for the first young woman that he met. Although, this dashing young wife hunter would experience many cloudy, and exceptionally rough days, his meeting Rachel would be his sunny day.

We all remember an old song that says: "Keep on the sunny side, always on the sunny side..."; this is an admirable endeavor. Jacob would try to look at life this way, but it was going to be tough. While Jacob dealt with Laban over the matter of marrying Rachel, he thought he had pulled off the deal of a lifetime.

In some ways he had every right to assume that it was a good deal. The glitch came however, when he forgot to do his homework. I have mentioned this before, but he neglected to take into account, the valued tradition of this family. The rule of the day was that the oldest daughter had to be married off before the younger ones.

I believe that it was seven years to the day, when Jacob reminded Laban that it was time to prepare for the wedding. Gen. 29: 21 will give us the details. I can think of no better way to say it, than what Jacob must have thought, "I want my wife now?"

No sooner said than done. That is how the dear old future father-in-law looked at it. Let's not waste anytime on this issue. The first thing he does is to make out a guest list. He gathers all the men, and together, they begin to make a feast. I think that it was going to be a garden wedding. Well, they have all made the preparations. The barbecues are all ready to roast up the biggest calf ever seen.

As I understand it, the wedding party may last for a week. One can well imagine the excitement of a weeklong wedding party. Everybody was going to have a good time, I guess. Apparently all is well. Laban did not seem to resist when Jacob demanded his bride. The gala affair had begun, and evening was drawing near. This is when Jacob would finally get to have and to bold his bride.

I suppose that it was dark when Laban presented Jacob with his wife. I would also surmise that the young woman was well covered, with a veil and all. That did not matter now. Seven years of waiting was paying off. The bride and groom were finally alone to share each other's company. Morning came.

The scheduled the garden party to go on for a considerable time. However, an unpleasant odor filled the air. When Jacob looked into it, he found out that someone had taken the roses away, and replaced them with stinkweeds.

Believing this guy is hard, isn't it? He had made the big switch. He had brought Leah, Rachel's sister to be Jacob's wife. How could he have made a mistake of this size? Were they twins too? Like Esau and Jacob. Well according to my sources, they were not.

According to the description seen in Genesis 29:17, I say that God displayed a noticeable difference, between Rachel and Leah. Rachel was well formed, and quite the young lady to catch your eye.

On the other end of the scale we have Leah. Leah was plagued with weak eyes. No mistake was made concerning the father-in-law's intentions. It was a scene from the past, set and ready to go for, "The Big Scam Two."

I wonder how often Laban and the others got together over coffee: Only to make sport of the fact that Jacob was going to get taken. I can almost hear the conversation: "Hey people, Jacob thinks I am going to miss an opportunity to get Leah off my hands." Isn't that something?

So here we have it, the morning after the night before. It had been party time last evening. In a situation where it has been party time the night before, the morning always tells the tale. The dawning of this day did have a tale to tell. For seven years, Jacob had been courting what he thought was going to be the breath of fresh air that he needed in life. She had made him forget all about Esau, and all the difficulties back home.

One piece of the puzzle is in the wrong place, and it changed everything. It was a romantic moment that had lost its romance.

For me to imagine the scene around Haran on this cool and cloudy day is not hard: Maybe it was, and maybe it wasn't a cool day. Still, one thing I know for sure, is that Jacob was not cool: He was hot enough to burn Laban for the deception he had successfully enacted against him. A very explicit picture is formulating in my mind. I see Jacob on the verge of taking Laban into the ring, for another battle of the giants. This would be the place to settle the score.

Taking physical action was probably at the forefront of Jacob's thinking at the time. He was tough enough to strike the knock out punch. Nevertheless, he would have added just another expense, which they would deduct off the winner's share of the purse. He would have lost Rachel for good. I feel sure of that.

I have often thought about this whole scenario. One thing I have always been in a quandary about is the matter of how surprise on this issue could have taken Jacob. He had eyes and ears, why did he not use them for their intended purpose? I am sure that the women were well covered for the wedding feast. That presented a reason for why Jacob might not have recognized the fact that it was Leah, and not Rachel. Yet that was not the only factor to consider.

Even if the bride were kept at a distance for the whole wedding ceremony, that still leaves the time when Jacob received payment of his bride. Did they not say anything to each other? At this point they were close enough to each other to recognize certain intricate details about each other.

Somewhere along the way, something should have placed some doubt in his mind about this being the woman of his dreams. We don't read anywhere that Jacob was blind like his father. So, how was he deceived? Did he just close his eyes to the realities of life?

I guess what it boils down to is the fact that this champion of the fight game had begun to throw caution to the wind. He had not gone through training camp for the title bout on this one. I see him as having seen the prize, and thought it was a given.

I expect that Jacob had accepted too many glasses of wine, on his supposed finest hour. At this point, the desire for the satisfaction of his bodily need was greater: Than the part of the love story where they looked eye-to-eye at each other and said: I love you. I believe that this situation must have been a parallel to the time that Jacob and his mother conned Esau. Esau did not check out the danger involved in only satisfying his fleshly lusts.

Well it is always in the morning, when the seeds planted the night before, start to bear fruit. Now is the time when we try to figure it all out. If only I had not…or if only I had…my situation would be different now. But's and if's don't do anything, at this stage of the game.

It is time to check out the predicament that he was in, and make some adjustments. Jacob did this. He began to figure out how he could still accomplish his goal. So, he made another deal with dear ole dad (father-in-law). The deal was that he should make Leah happy for a week, and then he could also have Rachel for his wife.

Listen to what Laban has to say: "Oh, by the way Jacob, just another thing that I want to tell you: It is going to cost you another seven years on the farm as my servant, for all the presents I gave you."

Well, now that the dividends for stealing the birthright were starting to come in, it was time to raise a family. Just remember, that deception did not die at this juncture. Jacob's sons were going to cause him the same kind of grief that he had caused Isaac.

Sometimes I am of the mindset that it has to stop. It cannot keep on costing like that. I am reminded of a scripture concerning Cain. Please listen to it with me. "Then the Lord said to Cain, and the LORD said unto Cain, Why art thou wroth? Why is thy countenance fallen? If thou doest well, shalt thou not be accepted? If thou doest not well, sin lieth at the door. And unto thee *shall be* his desire, and thou shalt rule over him." Gen.4: 6&7.

Life can be good, though some costs we have to pay are high. God will help us make life good, but some considerations apply. This is what I read in Genesis 4. Now hear this, don't stop here. Stopping now, will keep us from enjoying some key ingredients to success in life. God is going to make it up, for the costs we incur. Follow me to another consoling word from on high.

"And I will restore to you the years that the locust hath eaten, the cankerworm, and the caterpillar, and the palmerworm, my great army which I sent among you. And ye shall eat in plenty, and be satisfied, and praise the name of the LORD your God, that hath dealt wondrously with you: and my people shall never be ashamed."

Joel 2:25&26.

We can see, that the kind of consolation spoken of here, took place when Jacob reunited with Joseph. Much of the promise of this passage will not take place till a future date. This holds true for everyone, who has been saved by trusting in the finished work of Christ.

Well, it was not any different for Jacob than it is for us today. If we follow proper procedure with a right spirit, then God will send showers of blessings our way. The blessing I am speaking of is that of the good life.

The natural thing that begins to take place when we marry, is learning to live with another person: One with whom we've mostly shared lovey-dovey things. When we marry, we are placing two different personalities into the same bag. Then we suggest that we can put our hand into the bag, and pull them out as if it were singular.

Added to this we have the beginning of a family: Children begin to shape our future, as though they knew what was best for us. Again I can spot the principals of doing right, to receive right. I am referring to the situation of Leah, and Rachel both being married to the same man. Jacob loved Rachel, but hated Leah.

At this position in the lives of the newly weds, God showed; He was still in charge. It seems to me that God cannot stand to see the less fortunate stepped on. He allowed Leah to have children first: So that she wouldn't be put into a position where she felt the burden was too hard to handle. Jacob may have played favorites, but God balanced it all out.

Leah was keenly aware that it was God who came to her rescue. When we look at Genesis 29: 32, we can see this clearly. When I looked at the name that Leah gave to her first born, my curiosity is stirred. "…She called his name Reuben:…the Lord hath looked upon my affliction."

Leah felt that she was expected to have lots of children. By her ability to give her husband many children, she hoped to receive his approval. Here it did not work. It seemed to me that Jacob held Leah partially to blame, for being in the position she was as his wife.

I found an interesting article written by Tony Campolo. It was under a heading entitled: Responsibility.

The subheading was: Blame.

Wives feel resentment when they assume that they are responsible for everything that goes wrong around the house. They epitomize this in the television ad in which the husband is upset because there is a "ring around the collar."

The wife breaks into tears because her detergent has not removed the dirt from her husband's shirt. They see the ring around the collar as tell tale evidence of her failure. The ad never asks the obvious question; "Why didn't he wash his neck?" *(Illustrations Unlimited)*

Another article under the same heading of Responsibility goes like this: The Real Education.

"The man who blames others for his problems has not begun his education. The man who blames himself has begun his education. And the man who blames no one has finished his education."

Take some time to think about these thoughts, because they're relevant. Remember, Jacob should be shouldering some responsibility in all that has happened.

In the next chapter I would like to combine many aspects of this man's life. This is a guy who has caused me to wonder at times if he really ever met God. If someone had just told me about him, I would not have believed that he was a man of God. Nevertheless, since I have found the record in the Bible, I believe it.

So many sides represent the make-up of Jacob. It could not be that we are just like him, could it? Much more is still packaged into the jigsaw puzzle of Jacob. I don't know if I can capture it all on one puzzle. Well, we might just have to enlarge the number of pieces it takes to complete this masterpiece. If time will permit me some of your time, I would like to have you look with me at:

JACOB; AND HIS COAT OF MANY COLORS.

Jacob, And His Coat Of Many Colors.

Who shall separate us from the love of Christ? Shall tribulation, or distress, or persecution, or famine, or nakedness, or peril, or sword? As it is written, For thy sake we are killed all the day long; we are accounted as sheep for the slaughter. Nay, in all these things we are more than conquerors through him that loved us. For I am persuaded, that neither death, nor life, nor angels, nor principalities, nor powers, nor things present, nor things to come, Nor height, nor depth, nor any other creature, shall be able to separate us from the love of God, which is in Christ Jesus our Lord. Romans 8: 35-39

Chapter 11

When this chapter first crossed the path of your vision, it probably seemed as if I had mixed up my theology. I know that it was Joseph that had the coat of many colors. Although it was Jacob that made the coat for him, it belonged to Joseph because it was a gift to him.

Somehow, I feel that the reason that Jacob could focus on making this coat for his son was because he wore one himself. I have not found any scriptures that speak of Jacob, and his coat of many colors. Nevertheless, I believe that he displayed it hypothetically. We can discern a lot about a person because of the way they dress.

Many people exhibit their dignity and decorum, in the style of their dress code. Some dress in casual attire, while others are always in suits, and business like clothing. Some people's taste is more on the expensive side, yet others are more at home in the more affordable styles of apparel.

When we look at one another, for the most part we can only see portions of the makeup of each other. The internal plateau of the mind is where most people work out the most searching aspects of their lives. It seems as if the innermost feelings that people have, never come out into the open. Similarly, feelings come out, that we wish we could hide from the world.

In the New Testament we read of the apostle Paul. At times, he was unable to control some struggles in his life. In fact, he mentioned that there were some things in his life that he would rather not do. Nevertheless, he found that sometimes he was unable to master the controls they had on his life.

Just as it is in a jigsaw puzzle, so it is in the real life scenario that we ourselves face. I think, of the word many, and I realize that some puzzles have a hundred pieces, while yet others have thousands. Complexities make up each of our lives. Each of us would write a book about life differently. Everybody looks at life from his or her own prospective, and therefore they would portray it as they saw it from their own vantage point.

Joseph owned the coat of many colors. So, I thought about the diversity of colors, and the number of patches that made up his coat. When

I did so, I rationalized that in some way, they may have represented the changes that took place in his life as he grew to manhood.

With this kind of rationalization, I think of Jacob as the man of many faces. Jacob, the boy, was young and innocent: Until the people in his immediate surroundings affected him. We can begin to see Jacob, the deceiver, in stages. We can also see Jacob as the man, who tries to satisfy the wishes of his parents. In another segment of the puzzle we see the wanted poster, hanging on a tree. It reads: Jacob, Wanted Dead. Signed Elder Brother.

I am sure that you're quite aware, that this man's life consisted of many fluctuations. As we look at the picture of Jacob's tenure on this earth, we can see that he navigates over many pitfalls, which were easily avoidable.

Jacob had some living to do, before he could be all that God wanted him to be. This fact may already have presented itself, or it may yet show itself in literal fashion. I am not much different from this man of God. I think it may be a bit early to be calling him a man of God. Nevertheless, I believe that we ought to begin to think of him as such, so as too clearly see how the pieces fit together.

Some months have passed since I wrote: Part One & Part Two of this book. Now we are discovering Part Three. I really believe that I have had some living to do, before I could continue writing on this subject.

I can generally see important matters more clearly, after God prompts me to start writing again. This is when I realize that some adjustments needed to take place in my life, so that I could become more effective in some way.

When you're looking at me, or thinking about me, don't just think: "There is that scoundrel, a deceiver, etc.". Instead of being in this attack mind set, it would be better to think: "There is that man of God," and then begin to watch for the pieces to begin to fall into place.

I feel that this should be the standard procedure with every one of us. It would be a lot better to use this practice, rather than looking at the different faces of someone's life with a critical eye. I need to learn this lesson. Maybe we all do.

If I had stopped to scrutinize Jacob, the man, at anytime during his early days, I would have judged him too harshly. Often, I have heard my pastor say, " It is not so much how a person starts the race, as it is how they finish."

Many men and women have started on shaky ground, and then gone on to become people of special distinction, in their God given field. I believe that this is where Jacob presents himself to us as an example. Where would we have been today, if Jacob had not ploughed some fields for us, so that we could plant the good seed?

I have already laid out some pieces of the puzzle on the table. Many of them have already been placed where they belong. The entire puzzle will have included many action scenes, before we assemble it. The outcome is what really matters.

When Jacob first came to Haran he began to see some prospects that looked good in his eyes. He set his sights on these projects. What was the measure of this man to this point? Had he experienced a balanced diet of gains and losses? Or had the weights and measures been mostly tilted in Jacob's favor, to this juncture in his life? These are important factors to consider when determining people's capabilities for rational decision making on the big issues.

Let's just scan some of Jacob's life to this point, to give us additional insight. First, let's look at his birth. He should have remained inside for a short while longer. Instead, he got a free ride into life on the heels of his brother Esau.

Secondly, while Esau was out bringing home the bacon, Jacob was at home taking a more leisurely approach to life. He seemed to have more time to survey the possibilities of the future, for his benefit.

Another detail to observe is the fact that Jacob had his mom and dad on his side, when it counted the most. The fact that dad was on his side was due to the manipulating tactics of his mother.

When it came time to share the wealth of the family farm, it was Jacob who got the big chunk of the pie. He should have gotten a lesser chunk. The difference in stature from chief, to a servant, is quite a significant one.

Because of my evaluation of the scriptures, I find that it was Jacob that got the first all expenses paid trip abroad. Again, it was a case of a benefit orchestrated by his mother. If Jacob had worked matters out for himself, he might never have become number one. One thing that I have found, that could be placed in the loss column of Jacob's life, was the death threat from his brother.

I can almost understand why this was the case. As I try to balance the scales of Esau's life, with that of Jacobs, I find that I cannot quite accomplish this feat. Though I believe that circumstances placed Jacob in a more favorable light than his brother, I also surmise that Esau created his own end. Nonetheless, this did not help Jacob in rational thinking, when it came time to plan his future.

If I were only going to use a few words, to describe the treatment that Jacob received before he got to Haran, I would say, that Jacob got preferential treatment. It was as if he were born with pure gold sandals on his feet.

In a hypothetical sense I am going to say that this was the first patch on Jacob's coat of many colors. The color chosen for this patch would have been royal blue, or purple. I have chosen these colors because they represent that of kings, majesty,…

At the first major intersection of Jacob's life, he had to take on another color as the second patch of his coat. As he approached the well at Haran, and saw Rachel for the first time, I believe that the next color added was green. Green portrays the picture of vitality, vigor, freshness and prosperity. I like to suppose that he envisioned this at the well that day.

At this very juncture, Jacob should be expecting adversity: Just around the next bend in the road. I am not just trying to be a pessimist. When everything was just coming up roses, a distinct possibility existed, that a few weeds might break through to above ground level.

If anybody asked me to make a value judgment on his chances of clear sailing on the green patch, I say: Watch out. From the information provided to this point in his life, I would want to insert a large postscript. I would highlight it in large bold print. It would read something like this:

DANGER, ROUGH ROAD AHEAD!

If Jacob saw this warning sign, he did not give it much thought. It appears to me that he might have thought that the repair crew had just forgotten to take down the sign, after they initiated the repairs.

Every so often when I am driving along in the busy city, I find myself cautioned as I approach a green light. I am aware that everywhere in the country, they allow me to go ahead on a green light. So, I should not really have any need to be apprehensive, as I approach a green light.

I can see it from a long way off, so I prepare to keep on trucking without any apparent feelings of danger ahead, unless something in my spirit cautions me. This is the time that I need to be aware, that danger might loom on the horizon.

A few times in my life I have just about lost my life, at what was a right of way for me. It has been my experience to have someone come cruising along, from either the left or the right, at the intersection.

When this happened, the guilty party did not appear to have any notion of stopping, so that I could go safely. I had the right of way, but for some reason a caution flag went up in my mind, and I took note of what was happening. By making some adjustment in my driving, I avoided a calamity.

This person, must just have been daydreaming, and did not realize what they were doing. I have gone through a red light without noticing what I had done, until it was too late to change my mind. Luckily it happened on a morning when no one else was on the road, and it did not cost me.

I was at a function at our church a couple of years ago, at which I casually began talking to a man there. The next day I heard that he had died in a traffic accident.

The circumstances were just as I have just described. A drunken driver had gone through the red light. Right of way had meant nothing here. Because my friend was just going along without thinking he might be in danger, did not keep him from being dead. We do not know if a caution flag had gone up in his mind. Today we cannot ask him. He paid a high price for his right of way.

Well, I view Jacob as wearing this bright new green patch on his coat of many colors, with a feeling of dignity: Not thinking that life could change in a moment of time. I see this green patch neatly sown right there beside the purple one.

Jacob had every right to sew whatever color he wanted next to the purple one. Nevertheless, maybe he should have consulted a color coordinator as to the arrangement of the colors as he sewed them together. Otherwise, he would look funny wearing this coat: Don't you think so?

Even if the coat is new, if it does not fit, or the colors are badly co-coordinated, Jacob could look very silly wearing it.

I am going to add the next patch to the coat now. It is going to be black. Although green and black, contrast each other nicely in some situations, no pleasantry in their union.

Black has an opposite meaning to that of green. Terms such as calamity, humiliation, affliction, and...can be applied to it. Now, if I were the color interpreter, I may want to think more than once about Jacob's choice of colors, on this special coat.

As Jacob began to engage in the affairs of business, and pleasure, he was going to see these patches being added in recurring fashion. We see Rachel: She was the freshness of the green patch. Then there was Laban and his antics. These issues, coupled with the fact that they threw Leah into the picture, caused the black patch to be added.

No sooner was the green patch sewn on, than Leah (black patch) comes to haunt Jacob. In the eyes of Jacob, Leah did not add freshness to his day. Jacob loved Rachel, but hated Leah. Leah didn't make his day.

The diversity of color that I see represented in Jacob's coat has begun to interest me a great deal. Until this stage of making the famous coat of colored patches, I have used purple (blue), green, and black. Now, it is time to add red to this mixture of decoration, which was adorning the stature of Jacob. Why red? Well, red covers so much of the matter of which each of us is composed. I cannot exclude it. Our veins pump ferociously with a substance of this color.

When I think of red, I visualize it in the frame of one's blood boiling in anger. This visualization portrays Jacob when he found out that Laban had deceived him. The color red carries with it terms like selfish, covetous, and passionate. In your opinion, are any of these characteristics displayed in the man of God we are discussing?

When I think of man and his sinful nature, I put him into the color patch of red. Sin is like a scorching heat that totally swallows up humanity in its flame. Please read it in Isaiah 1:18. " Though your sins be as scarlet,...though they be red like crimson,..."

Jacob fits well into the category of the red patch, on his coat of many colors. When I think of all the hurt that he caused his brother, his father, and everyone else, it is quite literally true as stated in Romans 3; 23; "For all have sinned and come short of the glory of God."

107

When I look at these things in the whole picture, I can have mercy on Jacob, because he is in fact tucked away inside me: and maybe you? Yes, I would say that many red patches were found on this garment of his.

We can find reason here to allow ourselves to become hopeful. The next color, I wish to guide our thought pattern to, will allow for that hope. White is the next color that we need to add to the coat of many colors. It allows for us to think of ourselves as one day becoming pure. This is not only going to be one day off in the future, but it can be for all of us in an up to date situation: If we have been washed in the blood of The Lamb (CHRIST).

In many ways, I have painted Jacob as a manipulator, and he was that. He was also a man used by another man for that man's personal gain. Laban benefited greatly because of Jacob's stay in Haran. Finally, it was time for Jacob to decide. This decision was whether or not he should finally go out on his own, away from the man who was using him.

A decision like this was definitely going to present some grave dangers. Danger is a possibility, because everything that Jacob had gained was because he was under the umbrella of his father-in-law Laban. In the light of this, Jacob was poor. He was only asking to leave with his wives, and his children.

It was because of Laban's insistence that Jacob left his country with the riches that he did. By insisting that Jacob should stay for an extended time and work for him, Laban allowed Jacob to become prosperous. It was not his intention to allow Jacob to take anything with him at all. It was Jacob's craftiness that tantalized Laban's affinity with greed. Jacob made the man an offer he could not refuse.

When Jacob finally left with all the goods that he had accumulated after an additional six years, it had to be done secretly. Laban found out that Jacob and his family had gone. He was mortified: Not only because they were leaving, but also because Jacob had increased his own worth, by adding a whole lot of cattle and sheep to his caravan.

This had been done legitimately, through a deal that he and Jacob had made. It was not by particularly honest means that Jacob accomplished this near an impossible task. Read about it in Genesis 30&31.

In surveying all the incidents that took place between these two men, I would have to surmise that each got what was coming to him. They have both shown their ability to play the big con game. Each of them had made gains and losses. At the time of departure though, it was Laban who finally lost the game. Again, it was Jacob who had cause to smack his lips at thoughts of how he had out maneuvered his father-in-law.

I think, I would say that when Jacob left, he again displayed all the colors of the coat of many colors. He left with the booty of a king. (purple).

The threat of death was upon him at the hands of his father-in-law (black). Mixed in with these, and relating to the purple, was the green patch (prosperity). Inter woven with these three; we have the red patch (the sinful way in which Jacob got his wealth.)

We need to look at what is the best background on which to place all these colored patches of cloth. We need to find something that would enhance this interesting piece of attire. Putting anyone, or all these colors on a white background would be prudent. Similarly, it would not infringe on the rules a fashion designer would follow, when presenting a display to a prospective buyer. I suggest that all the patches used to make the coat, be fastened to a pure white garment.

When I bring in the white, I am looking at the prospect of presenting a picture of purity, holiness, festivity, triumph, and majesty.

When I think of Jacob's coat of many colors, I visualize a patchwork quilt. In years gone by, these quilts were popular items to have displayed on top of a bed. According to my taste, they were also very attractive. They do not seem to fit into the decor of some modern decorators plans. However, when I look back, I think I would rather have one of those old quilts than a fancy new stylish one. Those old quilts were warm and cozy.

As our children were growing up, I was thankful that we still a few old fashioned silver haired ladies around. One such lady that we knew made these quilts, and passed them onto our children. She did so simply because she wanted someone else to share in the warmth and diversity of color that these quilts offered.

The jigsaw puzzle is beginning to take on some color. The border is done. We have now assembled much of the scenery. A goodly portion of the sky and its diversely colored clouds is in place: Giving us a firmly interlocked picture. For me, it is a vivid picture of eternity.

As I write these lines, I have just admired the handiwork of God. The day was dawning. I observed the clouds, and how God displayed them. I have often thought of clouds as always being white. However, as I looked out off my balcony this morning, I saw clouds that were almost purple.

I saw clouds bordered with shades of red. In another part of the sky, an assortment of blues laced some cloud cover. I saw clouds enhanced with golden yellow: As the sun was about to surface over the horizon.

I believe that the clouds are white, but they take on reflections from all kinds of other sources. Fifteen minutes later I looked out again, and everything had changed. Some clouds that were purple minutes ago, were now turning to a lighter shade of blue, and headed toward becoming pure white.

The change was also noticeable in the golden yellow clouds, as the sun rose over the hill in the distance. This is how I imagine our jigsaw puzzle. It is not motionless like a still painting, but it is like a real life video that continues to give us the changes as they take place.

Put your imagination into motion and watch the changes that Jacob undergoes, as he strikes out to find fame and fortune. Celebrate with the young couple at the wedding, well maybe just at the thought of the second wedding when Jacob married Rachel.

Look with me at Jacob, as he is out working in the fields. Notice his face. We can see him wondering about the possibility of a future: Without out the perils of living with his in-laws. I can see him engrossed in thought as he is trying to sort it all out.

As I look at this puzzle, I see that I could not place many pieces. I have assembled sections by themselves, but they still need to be connected by other pieces, so that they are in their rightful places in the picture. The pieces just do not click together smoothly when it is the wrong piece that is being forced into the sky, the ground, or the trees.

When trying to put a piece of some person's tent way up on top of some cloud, it just does not fit. Trying to put a piece of the sky into some place on the ground, under some tree, will not enhance the scene. Nor will it allow me the addition of the other pieces, which really belong there. Nothing will fit from that position onward if it eventually becomes possible to make the wrong piece lay flat in the wrong place.

I am looking at a section where Jacob is looking at his coat of colored patches, and he is thinking aloud about what lies ahead: " Things are going to change when I get home."

As I try to rationalize with this man about the last twenty years, I find myself thinking: " There has to be a way to start fresh: To be able to put away all the wheeling and dealing, cheating, and frustration: That would be a dream come true."

Jacob has come to a point in his life where the fast pace is getting a bit too much to handle by himself. Trying to keep up with having two wives must have been a load to carry by itself. I can see him watching as both Leah, and Rachel wheel and deal, to arrange the portion of time they each expected to have out of his life. Each of them was trying to figure out how they could give him more children than the other.

This must have been some kind of life for Jacob. I see him getting home from the frustrations of a day at the office: They bombard him as he walks in the door. Sometimes I have asked my wife, to allow me to get my self back together again after a day at work: Before she unloads all horrible acts, the children put her through, in her day at the office.

I can almost feel the pressure myself, when I think about the whole scenario of his life. I look at some patches I have had to sew onto my coat of many colors. Oh, so you didn't know that I had a coat of many colors as well. Don't be too surprised; " *You have one too.* " Don't know where it is, search for it. Maybe it's stashed away in some corner of a closet, or in some old moth-eaten chest somewhere. Get it out! Have a look at it! It has something to teach, about the life it once offered.

Quite a bit of dirty laundry lies around my place sometimes: Before I get around to getting that old coat out, and cleaned. I could not find it under that pile. Some really rotten stuff was covering up that old coat.

What is it that needs to happen for any one of us to set out a course of action that will allow for our lives to be cleaned up? I know that for myself to get pointed in the right direction, I have always had to have a meeting with God. It was not any different for Jacob. Jacob's name was changed when he met with God.

Soon, we're going to see the white in Jacob's coat of many colors begin to stand out. Nevertheless, before that really begins to happen, we will see that this man will do some very important things. He decided to break with the past. He left the place of all his frustration.

Secondly, he made a move toward reconciliation with a brother that he had wronged. Once he had made these moves we can see where God came into the picture: To put His own hand to work for Jacob.

God began to put the pieces of the jigsaw puzzle in place. Jacob had just tried to make them fit any old place. When God took charge, the pieces were no longer jammed into the wrong places. God made it possible for Jacob and Laban to come to terms. He also made the reconciliation between Jacob and Esau possible.

If we are ever going to be successful at a new life, it is going to require starting with a clean slate. I see this beginning to happen. I am not suggesting that Jacob never faced another problem. Jacob would yet reap much, for the bad seeds that he had sown. Yet. I believe that Jacob was promising to follow God. Look over his vow, in Genesis 28:20-22. Then, go to Genesis 32:24-32. God had kept the promise that he had made to Jacob. This allowed for Jacob to be able to start with a clean slate.

How do we wipe the slate clean? Follow me, and maybe we can discover the answers together.

A Clean Slate

What shall we say then? Shall we continue in sin, that grace may abound? God forbid. How shall we that are dead to sin, live any longer therein? Know ye not, that so many of us as were baptized into Jesus Christ were baptized into his death? Therefore we are buried with him by baptism into death: that like as Christ was raised up from the dead by the glory of the Father, even so we also should walk in newness of life. For if we have been planted together in the likeness of his death, we shall be also in the likeness of his resurrection: Knowing this, that our old man is crucified with him, that the body of sin might be destroyed, that henceforth we should not serve sin. For he that is dead is freed from sin. Romans 6:1-7

Chapter 12

I suppose that most of us can remember the days when we went to school. When I think about the old school days, I vividly remember the blackboards. It was as if they were a big part of the teacher's teaching tools.

As I walked into the classroom as a young person, I noticed that the blackboards were always black. Blackboards should be like that when they are not illustrating something.

During the continual process of writing words, and then erasing them, the blackboard would gradually become smudged looking. Toward the end of the day it would not look black anymore. It was not any longer a clean slate.

The day would end, and the board monitor would look after getting the slate clean again. The next morning we would watch the whole process again. I really enjoyed the clean slate; assignments for the next day would not be hindering the view. No homework was good news to most of us. I have encompassed this whole story of the culmination of Jacob's time in Haran. I see that The Board Monitor has been at work trying to clear the slate of this Jacob's life.

For the most part the slate remained extremely smudged, because the pupil was not working out properly. Jacob was a pupil when he started this journey. He was still a pupil when he met God at Peniel on the way home. In fact he was still in the learning stages when he was called home to see the Board Monitor at his residence. This is at the time of his death.

When we look at our puzzle, and see the picture forming: Do you see the old schoolhouse half way up the left-hand side of the puzzle? Do you see it? It is tucked away behind that clump of evergreens. I see Jacob just going in for the days learning process.

Do you still recall the days when you took leave of your home, to make your way to the old schoolhouse? How well I remember some of those days in my life. Some of them were pleasant, while others were not memorable.

I do not know if you were ever confronted with the neighborhood bully. I had some problems in this area. The guy would never leave me alone. When Billy laid eyes on me, it was his pleasure to taunt me. Every time I walked out of the house to go out the gate, I would scan the area to see whether Billy H. was around.

Another bully complicated my life at the same time. His name is not readily available on the shelf in my mind. Life was surely complicated back then. I should just have been trying to grow up properly. I did not need this, on second thought; maybe it was part of growing to maturity.

I have decided that Laban was that bully. He was older and more experienced at getting things by rough tactics, and so when Jacob came on the scene, it became Laban's good fortune. For twenty years this bully took advantage of Jacob. Finally, it was more than Jacob could handle. He decided to do what I did much of the time, he ran faster than the bully did. Well apparently I had run faster than the bully had run.

Sometimes the bully caught up with me and placed me alongside a fence, or the wall of the school. It was here that he suggested that if I did not comply with his wishes in some manner that he would rearrange my face.

Maybe I was the only one with these sorts of problems. Do you figure? Justice prevailed from time to time. Every so often I had help from a knight in shining armor. Some guy who was bigger and stronger than Billy the bully, would say, "Enough is enough, leave him alone!" Well, every bully has to face the day when he is the doormat. The bully would either have to back down, or get his dues on the spot. Jacob had a buddy like that.

Take some time now, and open your thought patterns, and allow the word of God to stretch your mind. Mull over this part of the story of Jacob. Don't be in a hurry, but let this part of the account of Jacob's life permeate your mind.

Now, don't you think that at some point you would have told this bully that you really did not want to be on his bad side. Something had to be worked out so both parties could operate on the same turf. The alternative was that one party might have to move away, and face the possibility of it happening all over again.

Over the years of attending this schoolhouse in my picture puzzle, Jacob learned many lessons. He also picked up a few pointers from the bully on how to outmaneuver his opponent. When Jacob confronted Laban about the possibility of leaving to go back home, Laban reached out

115

for another deal. This was a big mistake, because Jacob's Buddy finally said, "Leave him alone now!"

Because of Laban's insistence on Jacob staying on for a final contract of six years, Jacob could leave Haran with more than just his wives and children. He became a wealthy man. I do not feel any sympathy for Laban at this juncture.

Things began to get a bit uncomfortable for Jacob after he began to prosper at the expense of his father-in-law. It seems that Laban may not have noticed what was going on, but his sons did. Ill will was beginning to show on their faces every time they saw Jacob, and they saw all the livestock that was being transferred to Jacob's side of the corral.

Jacob was a very bright boy: Though he had been conned more often than he wanted to remember. So, when he saw the mean looks of his brothers-in-law, he said: "I'm out of here." It was a major undertaking for Jacob to pack up family, herds, and all his goods, and leave without anybody eventually placing him on the missing list.

Jacob managed to get a three-day head start. During this time Jacob and company covered much territory, but nothing stopped Laban from overtaking the runaways. It was not any accident. I believe that God allowed it to happen, for the fulfillment of His purposes.

Without really planning it, Jacob was coming to another major intersection in his life. Nevertheless, before he could maneuver the turn, he needed to have enough power to make the turn: In order for this to happen, Jacob needed to make a fresh start. This is why Laban caught up to Jacob on the road after such a good head start.

Charting another course when we are still dragging old baggage is not an easy matter to accomplish. This unwelcome meeting was a chance for Jacob to begin with a clean slate. Jacob had made an important move in this whole process, but he did not do it on his own. He did it at the instruction of God. Laban also made an important move, but he did it with malice in his heart. However, God came into the picture in Gen.31: 24 and gave Laban some sound advice. Hear it with me, "…take heed that thou speak not to Jacob either good or bad."

Listen to how I read those words in modern day language. "Laban, don't you dare to come here with another one of your big cons. Another thing you should think about very carefully, don't you dare threaten my servant Jacob with any of your evil intentions."

After the old cheat digested this bit of good advice from the Board Monitor, he must have revised his initial plans. When he encountered his son-in-law, he suggested that it might have been possible that he would have sent Jacob on his way with his *blessing.* He implied that he might even have done it good heartedly. Read Gen. 31:25-29.

Apparently Laban had intentions of making a big party for the day in which Jacob and family would leave Haran. In my skeptical way of thinking, I find this thought a little hard to ingest. The only other party Laban arranged for Jacob, was when he switched the young women around at the wedding feast. "Jacob, you did not have to run off in the middle of the night as though you were a criminal. You could at least have come by the house and said you wanted to go home."

These are the words that I hear Laban saying. When I hear things like that I think to my self, Laban has never thought about anybody but himself: Not in any way, would he have let Jacob out of Haran with any more than he brought to Haran. Jacob's been listening to this long enough.

Finally, Jacob reached the breaking point. He has had about enough of this guy. For twenty years Laban used Jacob for purposes only favoring himself: Now it was time to ask him what in the world was wrong with his thinking capacity. Jacob's response is as follows.

"You asked me why I stole away as if I were a criminal. It was because I was treated as though I was a prisoner. I have been mistreated for so long that I felt as though I just came out of the hole. Then, my family and I were chased across the country, and my belongings were searched: Now, you have the gall to ask why I stole away secretly.

I served faithfully for your daughters. I went hungry, and I went without sleep, and I was totally consumed with my job. The thanks that I get is that you've changed my wages ten times.

It was not because of any kindness that you felt for me that you did not come here with an army and war against me. It was only because you finally got the scare of your life. God Almighty halted you in your tracks and gave you a piece of His mind. He finally placed you up against the wall and said, Watch it fella, you're on shaky ground.

Laban, it did not have to be like this, except that you brought it on yourself. If you had treated me with some respect, I could have come to you and said: Listen dad, I want to take my family and go home now. I am homesick, and I need to go back where I belong. There are some things that I need to fix up back there."

Whew, what a mouthful. I feel like covering in a corner at the hearing of Jacob's response. With that kind of response, I expect to see some kind of climactic result. If we read Genesis 31, we will see that this is exactly what happened. If I put it up on the picture puzzle, I would be putting in pieces that displayed an earthquake.

In my evaluation of verse 43, of Gen. 31, I see such a change in Laban. He has just made the big switch, from king of the hill, to lowly surf. In fact, I believe that I see tears falling from the cheeks of this father. He has just made the most profound realization of his life. He has lost part of his family.

In the process he has also taught the rest of his family a few lessons that they should alter some things in their lives. I can finally see a loving father coming to the surface.

I have for the most part been very hard on Laban, and he had it coming. However, there is always a chance that when God speaks to someone, they may reconsider. When this happens, it gives cause for us to think that we might have misjudged them. Or, if not that we have misjudged them, we ought at least to make room for the fact that God can touch anyone for a given moment.

Laban was watching a scene about which he was not particularly pleased. Suddenly he was watching powerlessly the chance of never seeing his girls again, and the probability of not seeing his grandchildren growing up.

The loss column on his ledger was filling rapidly. In recent years, whenever he checked with his accountant he was informed not to worry. Because of the vigorous labors of Jacob, he was doing quite well on the credit side of the ledger. So why worry about the day-to-day affairs. It should all come out okay in the end. It all comes out in the end all right.

This is a sad reality. The Chartered Accountant of all time will balance the books. I have seen a perfect picture of this in the lives of Jacob, Laban, Isaac, Abraham, Sarah, Rebekah, and on it goes.

Now that Laban has been subdued, he has one more deal to present. It seems as if he will never get out of the corporate train of thought. Thinking deals is all he could do. Nevertheless, this time it was a different kind of package. This deal allowed for more peace of mind, rather than a deal that would add to his wealth.

As I ponder the scripture in Gen. 31, I see that Laban initiated a process that was intent on looking after his fears. His fear might be that Jacob may take another wife. The deal that they signed was in the hands of God. Laban had come to respect His authority.

Jacob came to the table with an issue that also related to fear. He feared that somewhere, somehow, Laban would yet administer reprisals, because he was facing some misfortunes. He wanted a guarantee that would give him peace of mind over this matter.

Jacob also looked to God as the Watchman who would look out for him concerning the agreement that was presently being transacted. Finally the slate would be clean. The memories may linger, but the slate would be brushed to a nearly black finish. Each of these men would be rid of each other's intimidating tactics.

I seriously believe that Jacob had to attempt to please his father-in-law at this point: In order for him to have a major life-changing encounter with God. It was in measure, an act of good faith toward God, as much as it was a form of reconciliation with Laban. If Jacob had managed to out run Laban at this time, he would never have been satisfied to the point of knowing, that Laban would not yet seek revenge later.

If Jacob had decided to get stubborn, he might have told Laban that it was none of his affair if he married another woman somewhere down the road. This would have raised the ire of Laban, and caused a war between the clans. Who knows what might have happened.

Personally, I think that Jacob would have out lasted his opponent in an encounter of this sort. God was on his side. God had already promised to see Jacob safely home again. This took place in their first meeting.

Well, the bully was not going to be a problem again. The Big Guy had looked after it. God has a way with words. Don't you think so? There was no better timing than now, for God to meet with Jacob again. The stress of the preceding events would be enough to exhaust me, and require a meeting with God. I do not know if Jacob was expecting any more visitors, but he was about to encounter some.

At this summit meeting he was going to be there with his hands reaching out for a handout. It reminds me of Boris Yeltzin. Every time he meets with a group of world leaders, he does so with his hands out for

119

more aid. If you will go back to the jigsaw puzzle, you are going to find a large open area. This is reserved for:

The Battle of I'm a Gettin!

Part Four

Till Death Do Us Part

121

Jacob Bergen

The Battle Of I'm A Gettin!

And Jacob was left alone; and there wrestled a man with him until the breaking of the day. And when he saw that he prevailed not against him, he touched the hollow of his thigh; and the hollow of Jacob's thigh was out of joint, as he wrestled with him. And he said, let me go, for the day breaketh. And he said, I will not let thee go, except thou bless me. And he said unto him, what is thy name? And he said, Jacob. And he said, Thy name shall be called no more Jacob, but Israel: for as a prince hast thou power with God and with men, and hast prevailed. And Jacob asked him, and said, tell me, I pray thee, thy name. And he said, wherefore is it that thou dost ask after my name? And he blessed him there.

And Jacob called the name of the place Peniel: for I have seen God face to face, and my life is preserved. Genesis 32: 24-30

Jacob Bergen

Chapter 13

Someone once said: "Battles are won or lost in the trenches."

Ground warfare is likely to be the most taxing to the people involved in war. They are in the dirt, and facing the enemy in hand to hand combats.

During this process, a person may even be torn between whether or not they could kill if they had to go to war. A person really has to tough it out when they are in the trenches. The battle can be very real.

While making this comment, I am not suggesting that air and sea battles have differing degrees of exertion.

Nevertheless, in these situations one is generally not eye-to-eye with their enemy. In these situations someone might hear of the threat of the enemy and bombard him with some form of long-range attack. I am inclined to concur with the above statement of a war being won or lost in the trenches.

A tremendous amount of turmoil is experienced in waging warfare. Just to illustrate the intensity of this warfare, I would like to share a quotation from Quotable Quotations. Listen to the dramatic account:

"In memory's eye I could see those staggering columns of the first World War, bending under soggy packs on many a weary march, from dripping dusk to drizzling dawn, slogging ankle deep through mire of shell-pocked roads to form grimly for the attack, blue lipped, covered with sludge and mud, chilled by the wind and rain, driving home to their objective, and for many, to the judgment seat of God.

Twenty years after, on the other side of the globe, again the filth of murky foxholes, the stench of ghostly trenches, the slime of dripping dugouts…the horror of stricken areas of war."

(Douglas MacArthur, Near the End of His Life)

If Jacob felt like this was his lot in the last twenty years, he had not yet fought a fight. During these years he was in a continual battle with another human being. This can take every ounce of your strength, but it cannot

125

compare with the battle waged when one fights against the change from self to servitude.

It is true enough, that there were plenty of battle scares to show for the time Jacob spent in Haran. None of them were like he was to receive in his next battle. In the forth-coming fight he was to face an even more formidable opponent than he had ever faced to date. We are going to meet this giant in awhile.

During the time that Jacob lived at Haran he had served faithfully: Seeing that is obvious. Nevertheless, all of the servitude that he performed was with the motive of receiving gains for himself. Yes, he had to make a living, but he was not yet doing it as unto the LORD.

Jacob was a man that was not easily deterred from attaining his goals. He was just stubborn enough to insist that he was going to beat you one way or another. An incentive like that can be advantageous, but it can also lead to experiencing some adverse circumstances. Sometimes people have to be walked on, before they can attain to everything that they set out to achieve.

After the last stand with his father-in-law at Galeed (Mizpah, Jegarsahadutha), which means *"a heap of witness,"* Jacob was ready for a holiday. He figured that his meeting with his long lost brother was not going to be a picnic; vacation time had not yet arrived.

Considering the possibility that Jacob was mentally exhausted, some form of comfort would be a welcome sight. This is exactly what he got right after Laban and he parted company. It was here that God was able to console Jacob: With the fact that a company of angels was there to protect him. God had promised this to Jacob when he first left to go to Haran.

At this point, Jacob was able to set out some plan of procedure; that would make a good defense for the wrong he had done to his brother twenty years ago. He sent messengers to Esau, informing him of his impending arrival.

Jacob had learned to serve himself, and now he was going to start to serve others. When he sent the messengers to Esau, he told them to tell him that his servant Jacob was sending this message. He made a commitment here, but he was going to need divine strength to fulfill it.

When the messengers came back, they reported to Jacob, that Esau was already on his way to meet him. They made it known that he also came with a band of four hundred men. This was enough to send chills down the back of Jacob. Here is what Jacob might have been thinking, "I have as much as offered him back the birth right, by offering to serve him: Is that not enough? Why, why, does Esau still want to kill me?"

It was not the time to begin to waver in his trust of God's promise. Nevertheless, Jacob began to pray out of fear in his heart. He began to remind God that He had said, *"..."* Jacob put together a present that was fit for a king. It did not seem to matter if he had much left for himself, since he could appease his brother's supposed anger. Jacob probably still saw the wanted poster in his mind.

JACOB: WANTED DEAD.
SIGNED: ELDER BROTHER.

Life for Jacob was not going any to well, considering the fact that he held the title deed to the Family Farm. Jacob was in a real quandary about what he needed to do to get out of the mess in which he was. He would beg if he had to, he just wanted to have some peace of mind, and get on with life.

Jacob continually used the words "thy servant," to express the fact that he was not interested in ruling over his brother. He wanted a clean slate with Esau as well. He had attempted to make a fresh start, by making a covenant with Laban, but now he wanted the same kind of pact with his brother.

When Jacob came out of the womb at birth, riding on the heels of his brother Esau, he was hollering vigorously. If you remember what Jacob was like in his early years, you too may hear him saying: "I am not going to serve anybody, least of all you Esau."

By the time he got to Peniel on the way home, he had done a complete about face. In Genesis 32 he was once again hollering vigorously. Nevertheless, there was a distinct difference this time. Now he was saying, "I will serve, I will serve, I will serve; even if it means serving you Esau."

Why did this happen? How could it happen to a guy like Jacob? People do not just change, do they? It happened because God was directing the plot. Change began to take place because a man made a move in the right direction when God said for him to go. People do change just like that, when they are obedient to God. Everything does not get totally right overnight, but the matters of concern, do begin to fall into line, as time goes on.

Jacob had already decided to make amends with his brother, for the wrong he had perpetrated against him. However, from the reports that he heard from his messengers it seemed as if Esau had not yet forgiven his brother. In the mind of Jacob it meant war, when the messengers said that Esau had four hundred men with him. He was headed Jacob's way.

Jacob was filled with fear. Something would have to alter the circumstances for him. What would it take for him to have the victory? He would need to have an encounter with God again. I have found that some of the most life changing things have happened in my life, in times when I have been alone. When I have pushed aside everything else and taken time to be in the presence of God, I've been strengthened.

Jacob had already thought out every conceivable angle to this whole scenario. There was nothing else to do; so he put some space between himself and everyone else. It was at this special place that Jacob would have the greatest battle of his life. He was about to embark on:

THE BATTLE OF I'M A GETTIN!

To have a battle, we are going to need an opponent. I mentioned earlier that Jacob was going to be battle scared by a more formidable enemy than he had ever faced before. Now that he was alone, he was going to face the giant head on.

Have you ever watched wrestling, either in person, or on television? If you have, you will be aware that they never go on all night. One wrestler may fight for a half hour. If one wrestler fought for an hour, it would seem to me to be quite a test of endurance. Imagine for yourself, how long you could engage an opponent in a wrestling match. If you thought yourself to be really tough, you may envision a match lasting a couple of hours. Is that not a fair evaluation?

Well, here we have Jacob and the Giant. No, I do not have it mixed up. It is not David and the Giant. I see it as Jacob and God. If God is not a Giant, then I do not know anybody who could qualify.

According to my records, we have just begun to watch a match that is going to go on all night. Can you stay up for this kind of fight? Have you got your sights set on the scene? You are remembering the picture puzzle, onto which we are placing these events, aren't you? If you're not, you are going to miss one great match. I would bill this one as:

A NIGHT AT THE FIGHTS.

These two combatants were both heavy weights. The funny thing was that no one seemed to know the name of the other guy they were embattled with. They fought, and fought, and fought some more. If you watched it, it likely seemed as if it were never going to end. Maybe the only thing that kept you glued to the scene, was Jacobs shouting match with his foe: "I am not going to quit, not until you guarantee me the whole winner's purse. I'm going to beat you. You might as well get that through your head."

Even after Jacob's opponent landed a crushing blow to Jacob's thigh, almost incapacitating him, Jacob somehow fought on. It was coming near daybreak when the other man finally said "Okay already: What is your name anyhow?" Jacob's reply was: MY NAME IS JACOB!

Do you realize what happened when Jacob said that? He was admitting to the fact that he was a rotten, no-good sinner. In essence he said, "I am a deceiver. I am a real cheater. I ripped off my own brother. I deceived my dear blind old dad. I am sorry! BLESS ME! BLESS ME! FORGIVE ME!"

Right now I see Jacob in a crumpled heap on the ground. Sweat pouring from every pore in his body. I feel the utter exhaustion of the wrestler, as he now seems to raise his eyes to God as he forms the words again. BLESS ME! BLESS ME! FORGIVE ME PLEASE!

The other wrestler finally says to Jacob, "It is enough, your name is no longer going to be Jacob (deceiver, the cheat, crook). However, it is going to be called Israel, because like a prince you have power with God and with men, and have prevailed."

Bethel was the place of traumatic events, where Jacob met The Giant the first time. Bethel had indeed been the House of God. Before Jacob ever set out for the House of God the first time, he demanded that it was he who was to be blessed. You will recall that this came at the expense of

Esau, and at the great sorrow of his father. Nevertheless, he prevailed then, and he got the blessing.

Once again, we find this deceiver facing God. This time he comes as a penitent sinner and demands the blessing. He did not give up till he got the blessing. After the first meeting in the House of God, Jacob went on his merry way, and he might just as well have been saying, "Just give me Rachel."

When he went to Peniel, it was with a cry of desperation, and it went something like this, "Help me God! I cannot help myself anymore. I cannot handle it on my own anymore."

The nameless fighters are not nameless anymore. That is, at least one wrestler is no longer nameless. In fact, he already has two names: What about the other man? Something finally occurs to Jacob: He does not even know the name of the other wrestler, so he asks Him the same question that the other man asked him, "What is Your Name Anyhow?"

When Jacob was asked this question, he immediately gave an affirmative answer. Not so with the stranger. He just says: "Why do you want to know?" Then he went on to bless him.

When the lights finally came on, he must have thought to himself, "I have just been in a physical conflict with God. I have literally had my hands on God." If you thought that the injury to his thigh was a blow, imagine what a crushing blow this bit of news was to him: When he finally realized who his opponent was in this wrestling match.

Jacob could not get over the fact that he'd had this type of encounter with God, and he was going to live to tell about it. Not only was he going to be able to tell about it, but he was also going to live with a new name, and a new life was his at last.

Twice now, Jacob has had the slate brushed clean. Once it was in his experiences with Laban, and now it was in his experiences with his Maker. It seems to me that he is on the right track. It seems as if there are times when circumstances in our lives, come in three's. I wonder if there would be another blackboard, or slate that would come clean in the future? I think so. The latest event was the second of the three that were necessary to get back home again.

Jacob no sooner gets through the BATTLE OF I'M A GETTIN, and he got. He got the blessing all right, and now he got another shot at what he thought might be trouble. He looked up and away from Bethel and he saw Esau and company. Jacob arranges his family in a way that puts the ones least important to him in the front of the pack. Then at the tail end he puts Rachel and her son. This does not make Jacob appear as though he loves anyone but Rachel. "Jacob loved Rachel, and hated Leah."

Think about it for a minute: You and your family are out on a hike in the mountains, and you come across a pack of wolves. The way things are situated; you are encamped at the edge of a crevasse; if danger approached, you would have no options but to march into the direction of that danger to save the lives of your family.

So, your family consists of a dozen or so people: After you have put yourself at the front of the pack, which goes second? Do you put your favorite child second, so that he or she will be second in line to be devoured by a hungry pack of wolves?

I suggest that the last in line has many more chances of staying alive than the first few in the group. The first in line in any ground warfare are in greater danger than the ones further down the line. So, this is the question: " Who do you love the most?" In this story it almost seems that way.

When I look at this scenario, I surmise that there was still some work left to be done. However, at least he put himself on the front line. Well it looks as if confrontation and devastation were inevitable. Either it was going to be another battle possibly called, " I Might Finally Get Mine: Or the final swipe of the brush was going to clear him of all wrong."

If anyone were calculating the stress factors involved in the life of Jacob over the last few years, they would have to conclude that he has had his share of it lately. I believe that Jacob must be looking forward to his vacation time. It must be coming up soon now. Jacob went ahead, bowing all the way till he got near his brother. There was evidently not going to be another battle. Esau had missed little brother so much that he ran ahead to embrace him. Jacob just hit the oasis: a breath of fresh air at last.

What a homecoming! There was hugging and kissing, and tears of joy: And a heart felt joy was the preoccupation of everybody in the camp. Look with me at this joyous sight. I feel as though I am right out there behind that clump of trees to the south of them, just taking in the euphoric sight.

Finally, I am getting a better look at this elder brother. Remember in the early days, how he was always out somewhere in the bush looking for some big game to bring home to his dad for approval. I remember how I judged him to be careless about his dealings. Inside the heart of this man, I now see that a spirit of gentleness also existed.

Maybe it was the long days that he spent looking up and around at the handiwork of God that found a lodging place in his inner nature. I don't think it was ever his intention to seek revenge when he heard that Jacob was on his way back. If I am wrong, just consider this one of my personal rabbit trails, and not an interpretation of scripture. Several passages in his chapter give me this impression. I see Esau asking Jacob why he sent all these presents. Esau gently says, "I do not need it brother. I have enough of my own."

At Jacob's insistence Esau finally receives the gifts. I really like verse eleven of this 33rd chapter of Genesis. Please look at it with me. "Take, I pray thee, my blessing..." Esau understands when Jacob suggests that he and his family will proceed at a slower pace. I see a key word, which I'd like to highlight. "And Esau said, let me now leave some of the *folk* that are with me." Genesis 33:15

Esau wanted to help in any way that he could. When the messengers returned to Jacob in Gen.32: 5, the emphasis seemed to be on, "and four hundred men with him." In light of all that had transpired between Jacob and Esau in the early days, one would expect these four hundred men to be thought of as soldiers of war; men ready to do battle with a formidable enemy.

Now, this seems to have been an assumption by Jacob's messengers. Even if they had been carrying arms, this really did not mean anything. I imagine that Jacob and his band of merry men were also carrying some arms for protection. Let me suggest, that all the bands of people who roamed the landscape then, carried some form of weaponry. They needed to do this so that they would have a defense against anything that might be contrary to a safe journey.

When I read the word *folk*, I see it as a more gentle description of the people that were in the company of Esau. In earlier times, Esau may have begun to build up a mighty band so that he might avenge the theft of his birthright. Now, twenty years later, when Jacob and company were on the way home, I believe that Esau had mellowed some. I really do not think that he intended to do Jacob any harm on this trip.

We have just looked at three major summits in the life of Jacob. Each helped in affecting Jacob for purposes that were yet unknown to him. Jacob could look back on the experiences of the past twenty years and say: "NOW I UNDERSTAND WHY."

In the times we are living in today, we have seen many summit meetings between American and Soviet (Russian) leaders. Each time the respective leaders assumed that they were both going to come away from the summit with some substantial gains. Although they were expecting gains, they also realized that they might be giving up some territory of their own. Usually, we expect to find a measure of cooperation from both sides.

In the GALEED SUMMIT, Laban got a commitment from Jacob, that he would not marry any more women. This assured Laban that his daughters would not have to contend with other women, about the rights to Jacob's time. Enough problems already existed over Leah and Rachel. The concession that Jacob got, was the fact that all the deals perpetrated against him would come to a halt, here on this heap of witness (stones). Laban would never again come up against him as if to do him harm. They signed the deal on this pile of rocks.

Next we are taken to the PENIEL SUMMIT. At this meeting I see a picture of God getting a commitment from Jacob that he will do right by Esau. I believe that it was here, on this heap of witness, that Jacob emptied his self-nature onto the lap of God. What did Jacob get? If he gave up his self-nature, what filled that void? I believe that Jacob got the best of the deal. My feeling is that Jacob was finally filled with the power of Almighty God.

Finally, we are presented with the ESAU SUMMIT. In some respects, I see this as the one in which Jacob thought he might not get any concessions. Fear was the antagonistic enemy with which Jacob had to contend with at every turn of events. Nevertheless, because of the fact that God was in control, Jacob came away with something from this summit as well. First, let us look at the booty with which Esau came away.

The presents that Esau acquired were incidental. The big prize in his purse was the fact that he got back a large measure of his self-respect. Are you able to visualize this scene? If someone comes crawling on their hands and knees, and calling you lord, and willing to give you as much as you can carry; would that not make you feel as if you had won the big

133

prize? I think that I would feel as though I was reinstated as the man in charge.

So what did Jacob get from this major summit meeting? For one thing, he got a chance to have the final smudges wiped off his slate. His slate was washed clean from the blackboard of time. With this, Jacob also got to feel as though he was finally bowing his knee to his Maker. We can pick this up on this final heap of witness. It is found in Genesis 33:10. Look at it carefully with me.

"And Jacob said, Nay, I pray thee, if now I have found grace in thy sight, then receive my present at my hand: for therefore I have seen thy face, as though I had seen the face of God, and thou wast pleased with me."

I feel that Jacob finally saw himself as finally vindicated by God and man. I think, no better Bible verse than the following, exists: to describe what he felt at this summit.

"And the peace of God, which goes beyond all that you could understand, will protect your hearts and your minds in Christ Jesus." Philippians 4:7 (J.B.T.)

Are you like me? Do you feel it like I do? I feel that there was finally peace for Jacob now. We can all relate to certain feelings, times in which we felt such a sense of relief that it was as if we had died and gone to heaven. Is there a better way to end a chapter, than to feel this good? I think not. Jacob went through the greatest battles of his life during these summits.

The Battle of I'm a Gettin was the toughest. However, he persevered, and got just what he wanted. The words still ring in my ears, "I am not quitting till You bless me! No, I will not stop till You bless me. If You do not bless me, I will go down fighting to get it LORD!"

Let's take a breather before we go on. I for one am exhausted.

Look Both Ways, Before You Cross.

For which of you, intending to build a tower, sitteth not down first, and counteth the cost, whether he have sufficient to finish it? Lest haply, after he hath laid the foundation, and is not able to finish it, all that behold it begin to mock him, Saying, This man began to build, and was not able to finish. Or what king, going to make war against another king, sitteth not down first, and consulteth whether he be able with ten thousand to meet him that cometh against him with twenty thousand? Or else, while the other is yet a great way off, he sendeth an ambassage, and desireth conditions of peace. Luke 14:28-32

Chapter 14

As I was growing up, I learned many important lessons about what, and what not to do in life. Some people think that I have not yet grown up. I guess that is a matter of opinion. You may not be a good judge of the truth of that statement, considering the fact that you may not know me personally. All that you may know about me is that my name is Jacob.

One major lesson that I learned from my parents, and schoolteachers, was that one should always look both ways before crossing the street, or a set of train tracks. I am sure that I was not the only one that was ever given this little bit of education. However, it was unquestionably sound advice.

During my younger days, I was a safety patrol at the school I was attending. Having had this bit of training about leading others to a safe manner of crossing streets, became an important entity in my life. Even today, I always seem to think about looking both ways before I walk, or run across the road. This precautionary measure has saved me some pains.

I am convinced that there are consequences for not proceeding safely. I would like to note some examples where a life was lost because something, or someone chose not to follow sound advice. One such example involved my dog. Dogs are no different from you or me, when it comes to suffering the consequences of wrong choices.

When I was about eleven or twelve years old, I had a dog named Dusty. If my memory serves me correctly, I believe that he was a golden lab. Dusty was one of my favorite dogs, not only was he my favorite, but I was the favorite person in his life. We did everything together: If I jumped a fence, so did he. It did not seem to matter how high it was. This very fact was the cause of Dusty's death.

One of the things us children in the neighborhood used to play, was hide and seek. Whenever we did, Dusty was always there wagging his tail at the spot where I was trying to hide. You may guess how good my chances were, of not being caught. The only way I ever had a chance of not being found first, was to tie him up, or keep him in the house. If I put him in the house he would bark till someone let him out. Then he would sniff around until he found out where I was, and he would show his happiness by wagging his tail, and showing the seeker where I was. I could not win.

Well Dusty bit the dust when he cleared a five-foot fence to follow me to the playground. He was supposed to stay home, but he did not obey me in this matter. Because of this infraction, Dusty got run over by a car, and death was immediate. The big problem was that Dusty did not observe the safety rules. Maybe I never told him always to look both ways. Animals do not seem to observe the rules of the road. This was a tragic loss in my life. Dusty was my best friend. Now, this was only an animal, not a human life. Let me reflect on an example of an incident that took the life of a child.

The next example, which I would like to leave with you, involves a young boy of about five years old. I would suspect that at some point in his early life, he was told always to look both ways before he ventured across any road. The grim reminder of not remembering the rules still lurks in my mind today.

This young lad, who lived two doors down from us, came out of his house one day, ready to have some fun with his friends. In his excitement to play with others, he ran out onto the back lane. You guessed it; He never even looked one way, let alone both ways. The tragedy of it was that he did not have a second chance.

When the massive garbage truck came trucking down the alley, death came suddenly. I saw a family devastated, because of the mistake that this young lad made. He did not anticipate any danger; he was just an innocent child who wanted to play with his friends.

I have no doubt that many others could tell a story of occurrences of this nature that they remember from their experiences of life. Incidents of this nature leave us with painful reminders. We need to be careful to be aware of all the possibilities, before we rush off to engage in some activity.

In getting back to the main character of the book, I would venture to say that Jacob might have crossed many roads in his life. During this time, he might often have done so, without having considered any consequences for breaking the rules. If you recall any of the incidents of his life at all, this is evident. Jacob just set out to take what he wanted without checking it out the danger that may be waiting to cross his passageway.

Jacob would find himself faced with making a decision, at many crossroads during his lifetime. If he had taken the time to use his past experiences as an example, he would have swerved around many disasters: and save himself a pile of heartaches. We all know the saying, "Live and learn"; knowing alone does not keep us safe from harm. The Bible speaks of observing to do right, as the path to success.

Looking back only for recounting an incident, is of little value. Sometimes, it may present a good story for the listener. Occasionally, it may point to us as having been a fool. We need to do more than reflect on a situation in our life for it to become effective. Using what we have learned is vitally important, to be safely transported into the future, with renewed strength. This will allow us to overcome the handicaps that we faced back there where we faltered.

Jacob came to Peniel on his way home, fully aware of all the mistakes that he had made: Of this I am visibly sure. When he met God at Peniel, I believe that he may have visualized a song written many years later. One line in this song is, "Leave your heavy burdens at the cross."

The burdens of the past were ensconced in the blessing of God that Jacob fought for. It was a battle for change that totally gripped his spirit: That is why he wrestled with God, and survived. If Jacob had been wrestling with God so he would prosper in the material realm, I think that he would have been beaten early. The fight would not have lasted all night.

I am convinced, that when Jacob remembered where he had come from, it spoke to him clearly enough to cause him to rid himself of the past. This is what I see, when I look at how much of his own wealth he was willing to give up: to make peace with his brother. The blessing he sought, was one that could cause him to face the future, by placing value on past experiences.

When I look at the picture puzzle that we are assembling, I see Jacob at Peniel: As though he was standing at the foot of the cross of Christ. He has just had his name changed to "Israel," and he has obtained power with God. When I look at this picture in my mind, as he stands at the foot of this cross, I observe something. I can see him look over to his left, and take a moment to contemplate all of the experiences he has just encountered.

The next scene that I see is the one as he looks to the right. Jacob is contemplating the meeting he is about to have with his brother Esau. It causes fear to arise in his heart. He needs a quick fix to help him face that fear head on.

I see Jacob looking up at the cross (the cross of Christ), as I feel he had often done before: Here he sees the blessing of God that he had just received. One look at this cross, and he was ready to look back to the right, and say to himself, "I am ready to go on, and not look back. I have looked both ways, and crossing over is safe."

Do you realize what he did at this place? Jacob counted the cost. Although he could see that it may be expensive, he decided to pay the price. I think this may be an ingredient that is often omitted, when people come to the cross of Christ.

Often when people come to the cross, the opposite is true. They look to the right, to the left, up at the cross, and then look back to the left. This is the place from which they have come. The cost is too great to go to the right, and to partake of the place of servitude. So they go back to from where they came.

Jacob chose to be a servant at Esau's feet. He took the power to do so, when he looked into the eyes of God. As Jacob looked over the scenes of his tenure on earth, he must have focused on some regrets.

When I survey certain periods of my life, I can easily picture the areas in which I have wished that I had a second chance. I believe that I would have done many things differently. I have reasonable assurance in my spirit that Jacob did the same. Otherwise, I do not think he would have felt it necessary to strive for the blessing of God. He would have handled it on his own.

When Jacob faced God at Peniel, he got the power of God to begin the changes needed in his life, to propel him onto the right pathway. Now there were no guarantees that there were never going to be any more regrets. The main thing that his meeting with God was able to do for him was to be able to take away the guilt for his actions. I guess we could call it the grace factor.

At this decisive point, Jacob had done his looking back. I feel that he had already wished that he had never stolen from his brother, or been involved in a plot to deceive his blind father. I would say that after looking back over his circumstances, he could see that he had paid many dues for his actions. This is readily visible to me, when I look at the wages he received from his father-in-law. Now was the time to look the other way, before he crossed over at the junction of the new highways, which lay ahead of him.

The first step in this regard, took place when he looked up and saw Esau coming toward him. Jacob had already set out a plan of action that he felt would show that he had learned something, from all of his devious schemes. His next move was to do something about it.

One of our sons is an artist. Sometime ago he painted a landscape that I use to visualize the scenes about which I write. I find that I can relate to some scenes, almost as if I physically standing there in the picture myself. Because of this, I often refer to the jigsaw puzzle. It is time to place another piece in place.

I can visualize Jacob putting his hands up to his forehead, like one does when they are trying to see something off in the distance. He is scanning the future. In the scenario I am dealing with, Jacob is looking past Esau, and surmising what could possibly be waiting for him beyond past experiences.

Imagining that he is equipped to envision all the disasters, through which he would yet have to live, is extremely difficult for me at this time. Most of them revolved around his sons and his daughter Dinah. Nevertheless, stretch your eyes really hard, and see if it is possible that he might have even foreseen that slot in time. If he could realize, from looking at the past, that a person will reap what they sow, then he should have anticipated these regrets as well.

If Jacob could have anticipated what the future may hold, chances are that he would have used wisdom and discretion: When it came time to set values in the lives of his children. At this point we can look ahead to where he began play favorites.

Joseph is the one to whom he showed this favoritism, and later he also considered Benjamin very dear. Remember, that playing favorites was one of the major downfalls of his predecessors.

If Jacob had suppressed the feelings, he had for Joseph, so as not to arouse the anger of his other sons; he might not have suffered the consequences of the coat of many colors. I realize that being apprehensive about every move that we make is easy, and this really is not my intention. The point that I would like to pass on is that we should look both ways, when it comes time to make major decisions about the landmarks over the horizon.

In my own life I can see how some portions of my life have been altered, because I have allowed the Lord the room he needed in certain situations: So that some important facets of my family's life were changed for the better.

Before you think that I have just reached perfection, think again. I have some distance yet to go, before I reach this status. I was going to say: "Just ask my wife." Maybe you better not. Let me take you to an interesting scenario in the matter of Jacob's daughter Dinah.

During the process of much of my writing, I set out on hypothetical ventures: To get a look at the other side of a story. Let me try to show how the fate of Dinah, and that whole story, may have turned out differently: If favoritism had not been displayed in Jacob's life, with regard to his wives.

Go to part of the scriptures in Genesis 34:1. As you read it with me, try to pick out some key information.

"And Dinah, the daughter of Leah, which she bare unto Jacob, went out to see the daughters of the land." From this portion of scripture I form two pictures. The first one that caught my eye was this: " the daughter of Leah." With this thought placed up on the screen, I want you to remember that Jacob hated Leah, but he loved Rachel.

The next picture that I would like for us to scrutinize closely is this: "...Went out to see the daughters of the land." In other words, she went out to see what is typically called "greener pastures."

Having briefly laid out these two pictures, I would like for us to put our imagination to work: To see if we could think it was remotely possible that Jacob would have allowed Dinah to go out on her own at this point, if she had been Rachel's daughter.

Personally, I find myself thinking that there is no way that Jacob would have allowed Dinah to go, without him being on her heels to watch out for her. I seriously believe that she would have been Jacob's pet.

I realize that boys were considered more important in the scheme of things. However, I still feel that if Dinah had been added to the list of Rachel's offspring, she also would have been highly favored. I think this would have meant she would have been kept a little closer to home for a while longer.

If you know the incidents revolving around the life of this young woman, you will know that when she went out to see the world, she caught the eye of the handsome prince. Because of this she befell the same fate that many a young woman has suffered out in the world. The sin of immorality defiled her. Due to this event there was going to be a tremendous loss of life.

Jacob's sons were not ready to let an infraction as serious as this one, go without major retaliation. It is like something I have heard said in the past, "You lay a hand on my sister mister, and you'll have to deal with me."

An act of immorality committed here. We cannot excuse that fact. The guy involved wanted to do the honorable thing and marry Dinah. This was not going to be enough for the sons of Jacob. They were out to get revenge. Whenever I look at life, I see that two wrongs have never made a right.

Well to sum up, these guys pulled the Big Scam three, four: Who knows how many scams they pulled off. They deceived the handsome prince and all his mighty men into believing that they could work this thing out peacefully.

The outcome of the deal came out in favor of Jacob's boys. They decimated the guilty party and all of the men in his family. The booty, consisted of all that these folks owned, including their wives and children. Nothing in this deal satisfied Jacob. This act of vengeance caused fear and anger to surface in Jacob again. Seeing patterns that continually show up on the jigsaw puzzle of this man's life is not difficult.

Sometimes I think to myself, "So what is the big deal about having your name changed to Israel?" We can attach a great deal of relevance to this name change. It is the whole idea of turning from self-help, to God's help.

I do not always deal well with this issue. I get my sins forgiven, they are cast into the sea of God's forgetfulness, and it seems that I still end up paying, paying, and paying again. Does anybody out there know anything about what I am saying? If I am alone, please let me know. I have got a spot picked out later in this book to endeavor to cover this issue. I will be learning much of it with you as we go through it.

My final thoughts for this chapter could be wrapped up something like this: "Look both ways before you cross the street, and next time the outcome may be peaceful, and comforting, like as if you just reached the oasis in the desert." So what's next?

Every time I think I am closing in on the end of the book, I see another chapter replacing the space in my mind. Will you stick with me? If you stay with me, I believe that something special will happen to you. As we sit in front of the puzzle on the table, let's see if we can't start:

Working on the promise!

Working on The Promise

My son, forget not my law; but let thine heart keep my commandments: For length of days, and long life, and peace, shall they add to thee. Let not mercy and truth forsake thee: bind them about thy neck; write them upon the table of thine heart: So shalt thou find favour and good understanding in the sight of God and man. Trust in the LORD with all thine heart; and lean not unto thine own understanding. In all thy ways acknowledge him, and he shall direct thy paths. Proverbs 3:1-6

Chapter 15

Wherefore, my beloved, as ye have always obeyed, not as in my presence only, but now much more in my absence, work out your own salvation with fear and trembling. Philippians 2:12

When I get up in the mornings to go to work, going on a picnic is not a part of my agenda. My plan involves doing a physical days work. The consequence of this is, that I get tired. By the time I get home I feel as though I do not want to work anymore.

Every evening I prepare for bed so that I can get the rest I need. The next morning I do the same thing, all over again. On and on it goes. Periods of rest do exist: These are called evenings, and weekends.

When I sign on with a certain company, I promise to do the work that they require of me. In lieu of that promise, they pay me a certain amount of money each week. This credit to my account is not a gift from the company. It is my just wage, for having done a job for them. I do not owe them any favors for this service. I just owe them my loyalty, because of the promise that I made to work for them.

When Jacob first came to Haran he promised to serve a particular employer for a specific wage. They made an agreement in the good faith. The substance of that promise was Rachel. According to the agreement, she was going to become Jacob's wife. This was not a gift, but it was the salary, agreed upon by Laban and Jacob.

Before Jacob got to Haran, he had made a deal to work for another party. This arrangement took place a Bethel. During this meeting, Jacob stated that he would work for this Man: If He would promise to work for him.

The subject here is the meeting that Jacob had with God at Bethel, on his way to Haran. You may recall that Jacob said that God would be his God, if he were provided for in every area of his daily needs for survival.

Just before this commitment from the lips of Jacob, the prospective employer had made a promise. God had already told Jacob that He would provide for him. He told him that if he ever needed anything that he was supposed to come right into his office and expect a hearing. "...I will not leave you until I have done everything that I have promised you."

A distinct difference exists here between the Employer at Bethel, and that of a regular employer. The One at Bethel did not ask Jacob to work for the provisions that Jacob asked for. He just offered the provisions to Jacob as a gift. In Gen. 28:13, the LORD says: "...I will give it."

When Jacob reached Peniel on his way home, he demanded a gift. He said, "Bless me." Again it was given without a request that services be rendered. It was a gift. An important factor will begin to appear. It allows Jacob to serve God because of his gift to him. That factor is love. Out of appreciation for the gift that this Employer (God) gave him, Jacob promised that he would give something back to God. Gen. 28:22. God did not ask for it, Jacob offered it as a show of appreciation for the gift God had promised to him.

Until now, I have not seen any mention by God that Jacob was supposed to do anything because of the promises made by Him. Jacob had said, "If You will, I will."

The gift was free. Jacob would always be provided for. God has always provided for the just, and the unjust. If anyone has not been provided for, it has been because man has done it to himself. The provision has always been out there for the people.

In Genesis 35:1, I see that God finally has a job for Jacob to do. Read it with me please. "...Jacob, arise, and go to Bethel, and dwelt there: and make an altar."

In this verse I see that God is finally asking Jacob to begin working on the promise that he made. In answer to God's word, Jacob began to work. The first thing that he did was to make himself fit for the Masters use. He got rid of the garbage, washed up, and put on some clean clothes.

In verse three of that same chapter he wakes up, and says, "It is time to go to work."

Keep one very important thing in mind: God has always given, before He has asked for something in return. Some scripture that has tremendous value in the encouragement sector of real life is this: "Come unto me, all ye that labor and are heavy laden, and I will give you rest." Matthew 11:28 Before Jesus even issued this statement to "come," He had already paid a great price. He had left the beauty of heaven, to come and suffer the afflictions of this earth.

I think that if we came to Jesus with our problems before we began to travail over them, we would have the strength to make it through the tough times. If we come to Christ freely, then when he asks for us to do something for Him, we will not have a problem with it. The provision has always been there first.

In the Garden of Eden God first provided everything that was necessary for survival. Then in Gen. 2:15, He says concerning the garden, "...dress it, and keep it." By using these words, God is simply saying: "I have a little job for you to do."

Whenever I have gone out to seek employment, the prospective employer has never said to me: "Here is your paycheck. Please go out and work for me: But if you do not want to, that's okay, it does not really matter."

If so, many people would just run around the country making job applications, and never doing any work (I might be one of them). The employer in the earthly sphere always expects something first, then he will give you something for it. So we get the job first, and work for a while: Then we get the paycheck.

When I think of God as my provider, I notice a very big difference in the whole scenario. I picture it this way: God calls me into His embrace, and says to me: "Everything I have is yours Jacob. If you decide to love me, you may have an insatiable urge to please me in some way. But even if you don't, I'm still going to set out a table for you to eat from, and I will give you shelter. You just have to go out there and take it."

Have you ever been in a great deal of trouble? It might have been in the legal sense, or about your heath. Maybe your big hurt came while you were rearing your family. Many more issues exist, about which I cannot to guess. At some point in the whole scenario, you became insanely thankful. Because of this you just loved the one who made it possible for you to get the help that you were in need of?

I have often watched a show on television, called Rescue 911. Many episodes portrayed people who were so thankful for the help they received; they just wanted to love the ones that helped them. It mattered not that it was only the other person's job to help them; it did not make their rescue any less important. It was the gift of life. It is just a natural thing for us to want to express this emotion when we have been saved from an awful fate.

While we are in this frame of thought, we should step back to Jacob's situation at Bethel. If we look at the third verse of Genesis 35, we will notice that Jacob is telling us about the time that he dialed 911. Here he got an immediate response. In return, he began to have feelings of love in which he wanted to do a little something for his benefactor. I can hear it so plainly in these words: "...I will make there an altar unto God, who answered me in the day of my distress, and was with me in the way which I went."

In my imagination I see Jacob walking along with his family on the way to Bethel. As he does so, I picture him saying: "I love this Guy so much, man, I just love Him so." Can you see it? It is written so clearly throughout those early verses in Chapter 35.

During this twenty-mile trek from Shechem to Bethel, I can also picture him looking back with sweet recollection, of all the promises that his God had ever fulfilled. He might have thought to himself, "If only I could write, I would fill hundreds of pages just to tell you what a great Guy this God of mine is."

In the last chapter the caption was, "Look Both Ways Before You Cross."

Now, I believe that I can see Jacob looking back with confidence; so that he can look forward with assurance that every provision of the past was also going to be his in the days ahead of him. He may have wavered from time to time. Nevertheless, I believe that he was also able to put the picture back into prospective, when he looked back to recall how God was there every step of the way.

Jacob was well aware that he had been the recipient of a major successful rescue attempt. Because of it he was now willing to leave the sins of his family, and his own as well, in a safe place. God would hide these sins somewhere that they would never be found again: Unless someone was out on a treasure hunt, and began to dig up under an old oak tree in our jigsaw puzzle. This is the picture that I would like for you to see, in my hypothetical characterization of the life of Jacob.

If someone was out there, and they found the fruits of the family's sin, it would not be considered a treasure. It would have the foul odor of something that had been dead for a long time, and finally found. Does that make you want to go and dig up someone's past and sniff it? I don't think so!

Yes, Jacob buried the old facsimiles of the gods they had picked up in Shechem. This is where his sons had made his name to be as if it were a stink in the land. I cannot think of a better place to leave all that rot, than where I picked it up. The big old oak tree at Shechem was the perfect place to drop off all the excess garbage.

One thing that I find a little disturbing in the whole comeback story of Jacob: It relates to his dear old dad. The thing that bothers me is that I cannot find a record of Jacob making things right with Isaac.

This is where Jacob began his journey into turmoil. It would have been fitting to see him back at his father's feet, without animal skins on his arms: In that fatal deception. It would have been appropriate to see him there saying: "Dad, My Name is Jacob. I am sorry I deceived you into thinking that I was Esau. Please forgive me. I wish that I had let God make the moves to give me the blessing instead of doing it my way."

I have surveyed all the efforts on Jacob's part to do something about the wrongs committed against his brother, and God. Missing from this vivid picture of reality is the scene of repentance at the feet of his father. The wishful thinking dialogue above, are words that I have to put into the picture puzzle to satisfy myself, that reconciliation between Jacob and his father took place.

The record of Gen. 35:27 tells us that Jacob came to where his father was in Hebron. Here we find that Isaac was now one hundred and eighty year's old.

Do you want to hear what I so badly want to hear? I want to hear these words: "Hello dad, it's me, Jacob. Is that really you Jacob? Yes, you can trust me this time, My Name Is Jacob. Jacob, you have been gone along time. I did not think you would be gone so long. I have really missed you son. I have really missed you too, father: I am glad to see that you are still alive. I have been waiting to tell you that I am sorry for deceiving you by convincing you I was Esau.

Well son, life does not always go the way that we want it to. I forgive you, because I also had to seek forgiveness often: Especially from the God of my father Abraham. Jacob, I remember the day that I gave you my blessing. I understand that you found the blessing of the God of your father. Yes father, we had a few meetings, and he has blessed me as well. He has given me a new name. I hope you do not mind.

God, your God, has called me Israel. I kind of like it. It means I am a Prince with God. It has given me a new kind of power with Him. It has given me a new understanding of how to relate to the people that I have been called to lead.

That is what I have been waiting to hear son. One more thing that I have got to know is this: What about you and Esau your brother, have you patched it up? Yes dad, everything is fine now. You can rest now. I love you Dad."

In reality, the closest thing that I see about this matter in the closing moments of Isaac's life is that Jacob and Esau are together in front of their father at his deathbed. It does not actually even say that Isaac was still alive to see the "two for the promise" gathered together before him.

If you do not hear these words, which I have agonized in my imagination for, please forgive me this small thing. I just needed to place this piece featuring the Summit of Isaac, somewhere on the table. I know that I cannot fit it into the main frame, but I will just put it on the side for you to look at. You can put your own pieces into this spot if you cannot follow me through this one.

The last scene in this part of the picture has the three of them together: Isaac, Esau, and Jacob. I have placed them into chronological order here; in a sense that is what Jacob did when he came bowing to Esau. Esau was born before Jacob so that makes it okay for me to do this.

In closing off the life of this man Isaac, I would say that I think he found joy, and satisfaction in his dying moments. The line that says: "…old and full of years," gives me one last hope that he died happy.

I think this way because it mentions both old, and full. The word *old* gives us his status as far as length of years is concerned. The word *full*, gives me the impression that something happened before he closed his eyes and spoke his final word. I think that he got just what he wanted, by having Esau and Jacob together at home for this his final, and hopefully his finest hour.

Much work has been done on the promise that Jacob made to God. When does one actually stop working in this life? It is at the time of death. So it was for Abraham, Isaac, and would yet be for Jacob.

The main thing that I have gleaned from this chapter is that Jacob was only able to do anything that he did on the positive side, by the power of God, and God alone. If he had never had the meeting with God, all the other meetings with men would not have been enough to satisfy his greatest need.

Next to the ability that God gave him, Jacob found the wisdom for obedience in looking back on life's experiences for help to focus on tomorrow.

Stay tuned for: More of The Same?

It sounds like the reruns are on. Well not really, but there is a part of this man's life yet to come, that parallels some parts of his past. In a few words it is, family troubles again: But with a difference. Don't stop here. You will miss the best features of Jacob's tenure. In fact the challenging sections of the book are yet to come.

Re-Runs

That which was from the beginning, which we have heard, which we have seen with our eyes, which we have looked upon, and our hands have handled, of the Word of life; (For the life was manifested, and we have seen it, and bear witness, and shew unto you that eternal life, which was with the Father, and was manifested unto us;) That which we have seen and heard declare we unto you, that ye also may have fellowship with us: and truly our fellowship is with the Father, and with his Son Jesus Christ. And these things write we unto you, that your joy may be full. 1 John 1:1-4

Chapter 16

It is a known fact that every year, the television reruns begin to flood the airwaves. Many serials that people have watched diligently all year long will now be repeated so that the producers can make sure that you did not miss any of the gory details.

Well, that is not exactly the reason. Actually, the television industry needs that time to produce another series of shows for the following season. So, the rerun season comes down upon us with a fervor, upon those who are avid television viewers: Whether we like it or not. Life is much like that.

The same scenarios' seems to present themselves over, and over again. As people grow older, the plot sometimes changes, and new faces are added: But it always seems as though we are facing the same stresses. Sometimes I find myself thinking, "Why me again?"

Why me again? I thought about this for a while and I think I may have come up with an answer. It may not be that profound; I believe that it's life as it is. I think that we face these scenes over, again and again: so that we begin to be in a position to make a difference for those who will come after us. It does not always work that way, but we are given the opportunity to be involved in the lives of others; so that they can avoid some of the pitfalls that we have encountered. Let's call it the little job that the LORD has given us to do.

I could have gone through life doing exactly everything that my dad did, just as if I were cloned. I am not saying that everything that my dad did was wrong, not at all. However, there are things that he did, that I needed to look at and say, "I do not like the consequences that evolved from those decisions. Let me have a crack at making it better for those after me."

I do not think that this is too harsh a judgment on my folks. They also know that there were some things that their parents did, that they needed to attempt to change in the time of their reruns.

II Corinthians 1:4-24 would be worthwhile reading at this time. I just want to point to verse four, to give the thrust of this passage. "Who comforteth us in all our tribulation, that we may be able to comfort them which are in any trouble, by the comfort wherewith we ourselves are comforted of God." (Or were comforted of God)

By reading the afore mentioned scriptures, I see that I have a God given task to be open enough to Him; so that He can use me to make some of the wrongs of life, right. If I allow myself to be His vessel in this regard, He will do the work through me. I see no glory for myself in this exchange of life's experiences. It is always, only because of God, if anything praiseworthy is derived from my life.

When I look at this exegesis in view of Jacob, I can plainly see that it was not any different then, than it is now. Repeatedly, Jacob faced the problems in, and of his family. They seemed always to be making the same mistakes. Jacob was included in this to a great degree. Then Joseph came along and he said, "I am going to make a few changes."

We may not see it that way right from the start; it ends up that he did decide to change things. Sure, he faced issues that were not his to control. Nevertheless, when he finally got to a position of power in Egypt, he could have returned to the father whom he knew loved him enough to favor him above his brethren. Joseph stayed in Egypt because he found out where he could make a difference.

I know that on the surface it does not look quite like that. The outcome of the story gives us the final details with which we can look back in retrospect. It is then, that it is possible to see that this was the very reason that Joseph was born: So that he could be involved in some changes at the hands of God.

When we just look at the immediate, understanding everything is not very easy. This is why we need to look both ways before we cross over the deciding line of all life's crossroads. I suppose that it is about time to call Jacob by his new name. Israel loved Joseph much more than he loved all the rest of his children.

From the very first indication of this fact, Joseph was at a disadvantage. It may sound as though I have got it backward. However, I do not think that I do. His father favored Joseph, and there were many sons who did not like it. In their eyes it was only a matter of time before they would get even in some way.

Though Jacob grew up knowing all about playing favorites, he did not take the opportunity to avoid that trap. All he did was to give himself an excuse for making the same mistakes that his predecessors did. "Israel loved Joseph more...because he was the son of his old age."

He should have at least tried to keep it between himself and his son, but no; Jacob lets the whole world know that he loves Joseph more. For this son he made a special token. The other sons would be sure to know that if there were any goodies to be given out, they were not getting any.

When something important is brewing deep down in our heart, keeping it there is hard. The Bible says that from the abundance of the heart, the mouth speaketh, and then the actions follow accordingly.

If there needed to be a change on this matter, it would have to come from within Israel. I think that he wanted Joseph to grow up just like him. If he did, that had to include all his faults. When I see issues in this light, I say: Joseph suffered the things he did, because of the grace of God. So that he would be a candidate for change.

It was not enough for Israel to show his partiality toward Joseph; in the next picture we see that God, wants everyone to know that Joseph is special to him too. Joseph begins to have dreams. This magnifies the stature of Joseph, far above his brothers. Dad did not exactly like the idea that he was included in the package of those who would serve Joseph. He tells Joseph as much. It is recorded that Israel rebuked Joseph for thinking that the dreams he had, would come true.

Something is beginning to surface at this juncture, something that would never have been there in days gone by. In Gen.37: 11 it says that Israel observed what was going on in young Joseph's life. Jacob Israel, realized that it might just be the hand of God at work, for purposes yet unknown.

In time past, Jacob would have begun to scheme, to make sure that it would not be he, that would serve his young son. Everybody else may have to bow, but not Jacob. The whole picture of him bowing down to his son was the same picture as that of Esau having to concede to the fact that Jacob was to be his master. God does the choosing. If He says that all the elders of a nation, are going to be subjective to a lesser figure, then that is the way it will be: Like it or not.

At this stage of the game Israel had learned a few strong lessons. However, he was still naive in other areas. He was unaware of the danger Joseph's brothers were to him. Israel's sons would be the death of him, or so it seemed. Jacob's sons took matters into their own hands when it came to the situation of their sister being assaulted.

They had just cause to be angry. This guy named Shechem was in the wrong, but they made some bad moves in dealing with that situation the way that they did.

When Jacob's sons had a quarrel with Joseph, they initially took it out on the wrong man. The result was that they penalized their father. If wisdom had prevailed, they may have come to a better solution. If they had talked to Israel about it, instead of making Joseph the target of their anger, the problem might have ended peaceably. These guys really did not have it together when it came to the matter of family unity.

We all know the story of how the boys put their brother Joseph into the pit; then sold him off to some traveling merchants. They covered up their sin by making dad think that some beast killed Joseph.

The coat of many colors was coming back to haunt Israel. Now it was blood soaked. Red was the predominant color. Israel must have thought that it was his fault, because he had sent the boy out to do a job for him. I suppose that the fault did belong in his field of play, because of the fact that he had played favorites. Favoritism only served to sever family relations, not unify the family.

I have usually assumed that a person could trust their own family, when difficulties arose. I used to believe that I could trust my kids to tell me the truth. Along the way, life has taught me a lesson in this regard as well. We all want to believe that our children will not deceive us; that is not always the case. My parents could not always trust me either.

Israel's sons could have been a relief valve for the pain that Israel suffered; but they never moved in that direction until Joseph initiated it under pressure. The self-nature was very real in the sons of Jacob. I have not found many incidents where I saw a kindness shown in the heart of any of Jacob's sons. A few moments of kindness seem to present themselves. Nobody had the courage to act upon any feelings they might have had in the direction of compassion toward their dad.

Throughout life, it was one struggle after another for this man of God. Added to the loss of Joseph, Israel soon found out that his son Judah was going to be the father of twins. If isolated, this is not an area of concern. The problem was that Judah fathered the twins with his own daughter-in-law. At the time, he did not know it was her. She was posing as a prostitute. Judah went to her in this scenario. This is where the wrong lay.

The birth of these twins was another picture, or reminder of the past for Israel. A similar struggle presented itself at the birth of these, Israel's grandchildren; much like the fight Jacob had when coming out of the womb on the heels of Esau. We find this recorded in Gen. 38: 27-30.

Pictures keep presenting themselves as solid reminders, to look at life from both sides. These may be painful, but they seem advantageous in some ways. This has been the story of Jacob's life. He probably felt as though it would be better if he were dead. His pain was greater than he might have thought he could handle.

It is not time yet to get discouraged. Help is on the way. God's timing has to be observed. Our timing is not the most accurate. "Israel could have saved his beloved son from one of the greatest pitfalls in his life."

When I first looked at this statement, I thought to myself, "If he had, it would have halted God's desire to present a table of goodies during the great famine." So in light of not trying to infringe on the work of God, should I not try my best to change the wrong in my life, as I feel they are revealed to me? What can I use as a benchmark in the whole matter of letting God take control?

I believe that we have to make the efforts in life, to make the changes that can adversely affect those around us. We cannot just continue to be like a long row of dominoes set up to fall in the same manner. What if the last domino (you, or me) on the row is set to fall into a bottomless crevasse: Is it not our responsibility to avoid that catastrophe? I suggest to you that it is our responsibility to try to change the matters that we see as wrong.

When we look at this line of dominoes, we should be able to take out one of the pieces to leave a space. This is how to stop the last one from falling off into oblivion. Making that interruption in the flow of the dominoes, allows for us to make the necessary change.

In this scenario, I see the necessary change as being: Take the last domino, which is on the edge of the crevasse, and remove it. In this manner there will be another break to leave room for God to reveal to us an alternate plan. This could replace the destructive one that has been set in motion by our unwillingness to be an effective tool for change.

I do not think that deceiving Esau was ever God's intent for Jacob, and his father. God would have worked out his purpose; without the deceptive process put into play by Jacob and his mom.

When the word of God says, "...All things work together for good to them who love God, to them who are the called according to His purpose." Romans 8:28, I do not think that it meant for us to let life get out of control: Without us trying to stop the damage that it might cause. I believe that God sees this happening. He realizes that we have not come to the point in our life where we are yet able, or willing to do something about it. He takes the initiative and says: "I can fix it up for you, so that the pain is not so unbearable for you."

The beginning of chapter 15 went like this: Working on The Promise. "...Work out your own salvation..." Then if we look at another scripture in 1 Timothy 2:15; we read this: "Study to shew thyself approved unto God, a workman that needeth not to be ashamed, rightly dividing the word of truth." We can have hope that God is merciful enough to bring healing to the fistful of errors we make.

Jacob, is in the midst of the puzzle that has the beauty of God written all over it. He has already made some moves that allowed God to dramatically adjust the destructive course; on which he was headed straight for the edge of the crevasse. We saw some of this in the scenes of reconciliation of the past. The result was that Jacob offered to serve.

I saw another glimpse of hope, when it was recorded that Israel observed what Joseph was saying about the dreams he had. This seemingly insignificant line portrays one massive picture for me, when added to the jigsaw puzzle we have been assembling. It shows me that Jacob had allowed the effects of Peniel, to make another positive change in his life. I believe that this is what it is all about.

So, when is all this stuff about everything working for the good, really going to present us with some kind of major victory? Should I tell you now, or should I make you wait? I think that it will keep for a while. Much is left on this piece of the puzzle. We dare not try to place it too quickly. I want to gaze at it a while myself; then enjoy the victory for more than a moment.

The next pieces will encompass a scene called:

The Chariot Of Israel, And The Horsemen Thereof!

The Chariot of Israel, And the Horsemen Thereof!

For we know that the whole creation groaneth and travaileth in pain together until now. And not only they, but ourselves also, which have the firstfruits of the Spirit, even we ourselves groan within ourselves, waiting for the adoption, to wit, the redemption of our body. For we are saved by hope: but hope that is seen is not hope: for what a man seeth, why doth he yet hope for? But if we hope for that we see not, then do we with patience wait for it. Romans 8:22-25

Chapter 17

Some people go out on the town for a good meal, and they really go for the main course: Others find themselves waiting for the second portion, the desert. I for one, look on the menu to find the first portion: I would rather indulge on that, than the desert. This is the way we had it in our home when I was growing up. As a rule, we only ate deserts on special occasions.

Let me tell you a secret. Please, do not tell my wife. Something that I have noticed over the years is that my wife is the opposite of me when it comes to the desires that satisfy the appetite. If you give her a piece of cheesecake, or apple pie with a slice of cheese, then you will have made her day. She likes the main course, but she goes crazy over the desert.

When it comes to spiritual matters, I found someone in the Bible who liked his double portion. You should remember him from II Kings 2:9-18; his name is Elisha. When he went out on the town, meat and potatoes by themselves did not quite cut it. If he did not get that double portion, then it was not yet time to call it a night. The evening was not complete, without some of that Jordan Cream Pie. Are you getting hungry yet? I am working up a powerful hunger for a double portion.

In II Kings 2, I see that Elijah says to Elisha, "I am going to church (Bethel), you wait here in Gilgal." Elisha says, "Nothin doing: I am going to church with you." In fact he said, "Do not try to shake me. Wherever you go, I am with you."

Elisha knew that it was nearly time for Elijah to leave this earth. God had already spoken to Elijah concerning the matter. Elisha was promised, that if he saw the exact moment that Elijah was transported, that he would receive a double portion of the anointing that was upon Elijah.

So it was. Suddenly the sky was full of action. The Chariot of Israel, and the horsemen thereof, made their decent. They swooped down and picked up Elijah, and immediately made their ascent.

Elisha saw the whole thing, just as he had anticipated, in accordance with the promise of Elijah. The mantle of power fell from the shoulder of Elijah, who was up in the chariot, and it landed upon Elisha.

Immediately, he began to exercise the use of the anointing. It was so powerful within him that he could not keep it to himself. He got his double portion. Elisha had paid his dues. He had been following Elijah around, and one thing that impressed him to great heights of excitement, was the power of God that this man of God exhibited.

Elisha wanted the power so badly. He was so connected to Elijah, like grease gets into the cracks of my skin and fingernails, when I work on the greasy motor parts of my van. He was not ready to let one chance at that kind of power with God, escape his grasp.

Through the crystals of my imagination, I can see the correlation between Elisha, and Jacob. It began to happen at places like Bethel (house of God), and Peniel (the battle ground): The places where Jacob met God face to face. I almost get chills, when I think of such a power transfer to a mere mortal. Why should God want to endue a human being with that kind of power?

In Jacob, it is not just power with God that was exemplified. It is also recorded that Jacob (Israel) had power with men. That speaks to me of being in a position of usefulness in the eyes of God, and for His purposes.

I am almost getting the feeling that it could happen again today. I almost get the feeling that I would like to have that kind of power with God, and men. When I look at these men intently, I feel with my wife, in her desire for the desert. It is beginning to taste sweeter in my mouth. Just like a large piece of chocolate pie, topped with a double portion of home made whipped cream, or a Nanaimo bar (or any chocolate bar, hey).

Struggles and famine: that has been a goodly portion of what Jacob endured. In reality, no one is exempt from these toils of life. We must all participate. In some folks, these struggles are exemplified more than they are in others. I believe that this is because little jobs need doing.

These struggles are the testing grounds, in which God can sort out those who are willing to stick close, (so as not to miss a thing), from those who just want to stay on the outside looking in. Some people are going to be in a position, to catch the mantle, when the power falls.

I suppose that I never really realized till now, that the Chariot of Israel did not originate at the Jordan River, with Elijah. The story of Elijah, and Elisha was much later in time than that of Israel (Jacob). So where do you think the title of that mode of transport came from?

I am going to be bold enough to say that it was named after Jacob Israel. In Genesis 50:9, "And there went up with him both chariots and horsemen: and it was a very great company." Take notice of it, we find the mention of chariots, and horsemen, and it was Jacob Israel that was being transported. I find no record to say that it was the Chariot of Israel. However, it makes for some interesting dialogue, and it makes sense to me. You are probably thinking, "Here is Jacob, out to lunch again."

I see it this way: In Egypt, God put The Chariot of Israel, and the horsemen thereof, into place during the years of famine. It was first used to carry supplies back to the land of Canaan to refurbish the mental and physical state of Israel and his family.

I suspect that this occurrence may have been the first usage of this horse drawn vehicle. I believe that it was used again when Israel passed away in the land of Egypt, to take Israel back home to be buried. In fact, it may yet be, that there are many more times that this provision of Almighty God has been used.

I have got a slot open for another bit of my vivid imagination to be played on the viewer: I am going to formulate another piece of the puzzle in this space. I visualize the scene: As the Chariot of Israel, and The Horsemen Thereof, are taking the body of Israel, to have another face to face encounter with God. It was the same God with whom he wrestled with all night at Peniel. Only this time, he was being carried on the wings of God to have a celebration. Yes, I have got a spot picked out on the giant jigsaw puzzle for this magnificent picture.

In the broad sense, I see this chariot as the carriage that took many men and women, home to face The God of Israel: After their stay on earth was complete. Included in this list, are: Enoch, Moses, Abraham, Isaac, Rahab, and Ruth: and on we could go. You know something, the chariot will someday carry you and I, to our face-to-face encounter with the LORD. That is an exciting thought for me. I can actually see it as I speak to us about it.

You may think that my imagination is too vivid at times. That is okay with me. Nevertheless, I believe that we need to begin to look at the word of God with such anticipation, that we can see the written word as carrying this kind of excitement on every page. Maybe then, we can allow the power of God to send us out to the battlefield. Then we can do a little job for our master, in a real demonstration of love.

Pick up a book that has nothing but deserts in it. Look at the pictures in it. I bet that all the enticing forms of sweetness will whet your appetite. As you do this, begin to realize that the word of God is like that.

Sometimes we need something to whet our appetite for the word of God. I have often heard people say that they do not read the word, because they cannot understand it. I would like to tempt you enough to give you an unquenchable desire to devour the word.

There are recipes and pictures, in God's Book of deserts; for all that He has planned for our lives. Forgive me for preaching a bit, won't you? I just got carried away. I wish that I did get carried away, "By the Chariots of Israel, and the Horsemen thereof." The idea is beginning to look quite inviting to me.

Now that we have seen a picture of this Chariot of Israel, and the Horsemen thereof, and what it is designed for, let us look at how they transported Israel from doom and gloom, to victory in Jesus.

We have covered a couple of incidents that have changed in Jacob, as he became Israel. It was to be a process that would take a bit of time. I think that from his vantage point, he still does not see the sunshine. Israel still feels as though the blessing may have slipped on by him somehow. Nothing appears too rosy yet.

The sons of Israel seem to have come to a point in their lives where they cannot see any future (Gen. 42:). Jacob has to get on their case. He tells them that he is sick and tired of them just laying around. Israel must have had the feeling that his family was just going to die off, unless these boys of his went out and brought home some food. Hope has really begun to fade in this man's eyes.

Well, Reuben and the boys finally pack a lunch and head out to the land of Egypt. They have begun to run out of a few staples at home, and it is rumored that there is food for sale in Egypt. If they thought that they would just walk into the local supermarket in Egypt, and fill their carts, pay the clerk and head home: They were in for a surprise. It was not going to be quite that easy. It might have been like this for most of the people, but not for them. Why was this?

Joseph was the manager at this mega supermarket in Egypt. He noticed right away when his brothers entered the store. Immediately he had flashbacks of life back home on the farm. At that time his brothers thought he was crazy, when he openly displayed to them, the dreams that it had been his portion to receive from God.

They mistreated him, and they did everything in their power to ruin his life. These fellows were not about to get off the hook without feeling like

163

a worm on the hook, at the end of Joseph's fishing line. Reuben, Simeon, Judah, and the rest of the guys were going to be squirming for a considerable amount of time.

Joseph called them into his office. An array of questions harassed them about their family, and what their motive was in coming to Egypt. They were accused of being spies. The thought on their minds might have been, "We do not deserve this. We were just sent here to do a bit of grocery shopping, and this is what we get." It was not as if they were asking for a handout, they did have the money to pay for the goods.

In the eyes of Joseph, it was exam time for his brothers. It was time to take away all the notebooks, textbooks, and see what they really knew. When the testing comes, we are often in the disadvantaged position of having something taken from us. When it comes to exams, we do not get to use our notes, where all the answers neatly stored for easy access.

In a similar manner, Simeon was taken from their midst, to remain with Joseph. It was the guarantee that the guys would not just eat and run. I am not navigating through the whole story here, because it would require a separate book to do it properly. I just want to make the connections here to fill in the story of Jacob.

It is not as though the brothers of Joseph had always been faithful in dealing fairly in the past. Joseph knew that for a fact. He had been subjected to much suffering because of these trusty guys. At first glance, it seems as though he is out for revenge: To make sure that they pay dearly for everything they made him go through. Added to their already heavy hearts, he tells them not to come back for more food unless they bring their youngest brother with them.

This command was not one that would be easy to obey. Israel was not ready to let Benjamin out of his sight, like he did Joseph. It had been a very expensive errand that Jacob had sent Joseph on that day years ago, and the pain had never left him.

When the boys came home, they told their dad all that had happened. They made it known that the man in charge at, *Egypt General Store*, was not an easy man to deal with. They reported all that Joseph had told them, even the bad news about having to bring Benjamin back with them.

Israel could not grasp the idea of letting Benjamin out of his sight for this trip to Egypt. Jacob had written the script for many big deals in the past. He had added some great victories to his war chest. Now he was faced with a situation in which he thought he had no chance of winning. Would he indeed allow himself to be engaged in this affair at all? He was in a position of no hope. Every semblance of salvaging any peace of mind for his dying years was now evading his grasp.

Sometimes we need to be in that position: Where all hope of being able to handle our own situation is wrenched away from us. Trusting Jesus is the only thing left to do. I find Jacob in that state. He was put into a position of having to trust somebody other than himself. It did not come easy to handle a scenario like the one he was now engulfed in.

Well, after a great deal of deliberation, Benjamin was sent along, and I think Israel began a prayer meeting. What else could he do? When the sons of Israel got back to Egypt and looked to Joseph to relieve their pain, he kept them in the arena with the lions for a little longer. They still had no easy time of it, even after they had done everything that they were asked to do.

They must have been looking for a break to come soon. These boys were facing the pain that they themselves had inflicted on Jacob. The pain felt by their grandfather Isaac, was also theirs to share in this short story that depicted their lives.

Finally the break they were looking for came. Joseph broke down and told his brothers that he was their long lost brother Joseph. It was a near impossibility for them to believe this. At first they were in a bit of a quandary when Joseph identified himself.

The whole picture is unfolding like an episode of Unsolved Mysteries. If you are familiar with that television program, you may be aware of the many times that there have been moments of elation: When someone has been reunited with a long lost family member.

Joseph put himself at great risk by revealing himself to his brethren, because of the fact that the Egyptians hated the Hebrews. When Pharaoh found out that Joseph was a Hebrew, he could have turned on Joseph. Still, he did not. Why was that?

Joseph was a man who was set up to be the element for change. It was he who was to be used to make a difference. Pharaoh was delighted that Joseph was so happy. I think that it must have been evident to him that Joseph had been the product of a broken heart. Now Pharaoh could see that it could be healed. Pharaoh had a heart prepared by God to be a channel to allow healing to flow. This in the final stages would bring home the blessing that Israel had been waiting for, the blessing that he probably thought had eluded him: Though it had been promised.

Hope was beginning to show itself as a piece of the puzzle. Hope was going to light up the night sky, and allow the Chariots of Israel, and the Horsemen thereof, to come onto the scene for the big Rescue 911 call.

Nearly all the unrest was gone now. It was just a matter of going home and breaking the news to Israel. How would he take this kind of a major surprise? Think about it for a moment, it has been more than twenty years since Joseph has left home. Until now Israel is convinced that Joseph has been dead all this time. Now his sons are on the way back to the land of Canaan, to tell him that they had lived a lie all these years. Joseph was actually alive and well in Egypt.

Upon hearing these words, Jacob slid off the rock on which he was sitting. I think he was about to have a heart attack. He spotted the game they were playing this time, or was it a game? I can visualize him telling them not to put him through it again. I am too old for this kind of stuff.

It is stated that Jacob did not believe their story. Would you? For me to imagine this scene is impossible, because of what happened during the initial stages of Jacob's life, which were steeped in deception. His sons are telling him that Joseph is alive, and that he was in fact the governor of the land of Egypt.

I can see how Reuben and the others must have felt like pulling their hair out, figuring on a way to convince their father that this was no ruse. They kept on talking about everything that had taken place. Not a word of what they said was able to move the old patriarch. It was absolutely hopeless, that is until one very significant thing happened.

We have just seen the perceived deception, perceived by Jacob that is: It correlated with the past in his life. A new scene begins to come into focus. It is the future: It is part of the blessing of God that is starting to surface.

As I am watching, I am excited as this old man begins to allow a smile to light up a face that has lain dormant for such a long time. What is it that caused such a change? It had to be something of an earth shattering nature. In the later part of Genesis 45:27 it says:

"When he saw the wagons, which Joseph had sent to carry him, the spirit of Jacob their father revived."

I have just allowed my imagination to go into the search mode, and it has come to an abrupt halt in front of the home of Israel. A party was now in full force. People were shouting with excitement; they were dancing with glee. One sight that really caught my eye was when I saw this elderly, very reserved gentleman, jumping around the place. It was a vivid sight of vivacity.

It was Israel.

The delay in the fulfillment of promises had caused him to doubt nearly everything. Nevertheless, now, when he saw the wagons, he can finally see the fruit of the words that he had heard. Yes, I think that this was the fruit being received; concerning the words he had heard from God. "In thee, and thy seed, shall all the nations of the earth be blessed."

In the mind of Israel, it was in Joseph where his hopes for this fulfillment were going to take place. It was all initiated in the way that Jacob felt about Rachel. Jacob loved Rachel, and Joseph was her son. I can see how the birthing of nations required an act of love, in the eyes of this man. Now he can see clearly.

As Israel saw the wagons which pharaoh sent, I see him straining his eyes: Which were already going somewhat dim. It is as though he is really trying to focus on something off behind the wagonloads of supplies.

Yes, yes! It was the Chariot of Israel, and The Horsemen Thereof. They were hanging around to see that everything was going on schedule, for the time that Israel would need his final carriage ride: The ride where he would once again come face to face, with the one he had wrestled with to obtain favor.

In response to all that has happened, it seemed to Jacob that no one is working fast enough to pack the luggage. It was as though the wagons were not being loaded quickly enough. When Jacob finally saw the light, he said, "I will go." Is it not something to behold, when you see hope built up in a person? Once again they can say, "I Can Do It!

I Can Do It!"

Without hope, all Jacob was ever able to see was that he was going to die in despair. He was not going to be able to pass the blessing on in love. Both of the ones he had loved were gone. Jacob had committed himself to go to see Joseph. In Jacob's heart there seemed to be a little apprehension about the journey.

It is good to have a back up. The Guy that has been Jacob's biggest back up of all time, appeared to him again; He had often done so in past. He called him saying, "Jacob, Jacob."

Jacob answered and said, "Here I am." The Mighty Consoler said to him, "Fear not; I will be with you."

Take A Break

Part B.

The Double Portion

For his anger endureth but for a moment; in His favor is life: weeping may endure for a night, but joy cometh in the morning. Psalms 30:5

As I read this passage of scripture, a picture came to my mind for the closing scenes of Israel's life. It is a picture of a past that has been full of hurt, and weeping. Joy has been the furthest thing from Jacobs reach. However, now, as they approach Egypt, their lives are about to change.

A while back, I wondered when the victory of all things having worked for the good, was going to arrive. Now is the time. I can see the entire family of Israel encamped at Goshen. Israel has not slept all night. He has sent word ahead to tell Joseph that he was waiting at Goshen. As the sun peeked up over the horizon, Joseph was en route to victory head quarters. Joseph brought a package with him. This package would be the one for which Jacob had been waiting.

As Joseph approaches the town of Goshen, he also is filled with anticipation. It has been a struggle for him as well. As he ran into the presence of his father, he hung the package around his father's neck. The package was, the arms of Joseph, he was the package of joy.

Joy Comes in The Morning.

Now Jacob was so happy that he could die. At least this is the way that he had it pegged. But do you realize that this occasion of victory in Jesus, added another seventeen years to Israel's life? It is amazing what a little joy can do, is it not.

It was not quite the right time for this old fellow to leave this earth. The blessing that he had received from his father Isaac, was transitional. It could not be kept by the one to whom it was given. Israel was going to have to pass it on. It is after all; better to give than to receive.

In order for him to pass the blessing on, Israel needed to adopt a couple of lads. They were the sons of Joseph. Their names were, Ephraim, and Manasseh. Jacob took these two lads and blessed them. In this whole process Jacob got a double portion. It was like when Elisha got his double portion. It happened when he saw something happen.

For Elisha it was when he saw Elijah transported by the Chariot of Israel. Now, for Israel his double portion came when he saw Joseph's sons. Israel's first portion was his own sons'. His second portion: Ephraim and Manasseh made up the double portion.

Before Israel dies he has another job to do. He has a few gifts to pass on to the rest of his children. Each of them got what had been coming to them. Some of the boys may not have been all that excited about their portion, but it was their father's right to give it to them. You can find the record of the last few transactions recorded in Genesis 48&49.

When I was younger, and still living at home, our family often assembled jigsaw puzzles. When it looked as though it was nearing completion, I would try to put aside a piece that I thought would be the last piece. I would hide that piece, so that I could put the last piece in its proper place. For some reason this was my pleasure.

I have got that piece in my hand right now. I have hung onto it for quite some time. Now I will place it on the table and finish off this puzzle of Jacob's life. It has been kind of hard to assemble this jigsaw puzzle because this puzzle has been a motion picture. It was not a still life portrait. Jacob was a man of action.

It is hard to steady my hands enough, to be able to put this last piece into the last jagged hole, in the whole picture we have been working on. However, I am glad that I can have the privilege of sliding this piece across the table and snapping it into the final open space.

Here goes. The Chariot that has been waiting in the wings is on its way. I can hear the rushing sounds as it picks up speed to reach its destination. It had to make a pick up in Egypt. It happened suddenly, just like it would with Elijah: In an instant Israel was gone. Swooped up by, **THE CHARIOT OF ISRAEL, AND THE HORSEMEN THEREOF!**

The assignment of this entourage of angels was to make a short stop in the land of Canaan, to drop off the body of Israel. Then, the last stop was to be reserved for the two combatants at Peniel.

It was coming near daybreak, when the Chariot of Israel pulled up to the foot of "THE THRONE OF GOD." It was Joy in the Morning, when Jacob finally answered to the name of ISRAEL in the home of THE KING OF ISRAEL.

When Jacob and God met at Peniel, it was the scene of confrontation for change to take place in Jacob's life. The scene I see now is one of total submission. I am reminded of the parable of the prodigal son, where I read the part that made a particular impact on me this morning. It goes like this: "…the son said unto him, Father, I have sinned against heaven, and in thy sight, and am no more worthy to be called thy son. But the father said to

171

his servants, bring forth the best robe, and put it on him. Put a ring on his hand, and shoes on his feet. And bring hither the fatted calf, and kill it, and let us eat, and be merry." Luke 15:21-24

"And, yes you are worthy to be called my son, Israel."

This has been Jacob Israel's short story. The details have often been placed in somewhat of a hypothetical manner, rather than in the actual way they were recorded in scripture.

The reason I have done this, is so that we can grasp the content of what Jacob went through, and understand it in the light of the times that we are living in today. Often, people do not understand the language used in the days in which these ancient men of the Bible lived. Some people think that these people were only figments of someone's imagination.

Because of this, they may not have looked at a text and seen the full meaning of what was really said. By putting it in terms we use today, many of us may come to a better understanding of how to search each individual line for some meaning that will affects us for change.

I have never intentionally tried to be irreverent during my exegesis. Sometimes the usage of my language may have made it appear as though I had done that. If I have offended anyone in this manner, please forgive me. My heart has been to display this account of the character of Jacob, as much as possible, in really modern day understandable ways.

In the next section I want to let you have a little look at the short story that depicts my jigsaw puzzle. Then in closing I would like you to look at yours. Will you stay tuned for the finish? You may find that there is not much of a difference between Jacob Israel, and you and I.

We are coming to the last few pieces, yours and mine: Each of us in our own puzzle yet intertwined with each other's puzzle.

Part Five

A Couple of Short Stories

Jacob Bergen

Well, My Name Is Jacob!

Jacob Israel and I, have some things in common, it's the following.

And Jacob was left alone; and there wrestled a man with him until the breaking of the day. And when he saw that he prevailed not against him, he touched the hollow of his thigh; and the hollow of Jacob's thigh was out of joint, as he wrestled with him. And he said, Let me go, for the day breaketh. And he said, I will not let thee go, except thou bless me. And he said unto him, What *is* thy name? And he said, Jacob. And he said, Thy name shall be called no more Jacob, but Israel: for as a prince hast thou power with God and with men, and hast prevailed.

Genesis 32 24-28

Jacob Bergen

Chapter 18

When I make the analogy with the Jacob of the Bible, to myself; it seems to me as though his story was a more valuable lesson in living, than that of my own. This comparison may hold true for you as well, because of the lessons for living God presents to us in the Bible.

We often revere people of the Bible because of their exploits, and I trust that this is only fitting. I expect it is a part of the plan of God, but so are we.

The people of the Bible had the same humanity as we do. Their chances of ever seeing God face to face were no better than ours. At first glance it would appear as though this could not be the case.

How many people have been on the mountaintop and seen the burning bush, like Moses? How many folks do you know of who have had a physical wrestling match with the Almighty? How many people in our world have been ejected from our world in a heavenly chariot, like Elijah? I do not know of any.

Just because God displayed His power in the lives of these archaic folks, does not mean that they were turned into divine beings. You or I could just as easily have been placed into those time frames of history, and been a Moses, Jacob, or a Rachel. However, God chose to have each of us in our own space in time.

One day when the books are opened around God's throne, the chronology of people, and events, will continue from John, in Revelation, to include Martin Luther, John and Charles Wesley, Billy Graham, Chuck Colson, Queen Elizabeth, David Mainse, you and me. The Book of Life will be all-inclusive.

If this is the case, then each of our lives will be shown to have been important, like a set of chess pieces in play: In the context of the whole picture. I will have my short story, and you will have yours. Let's have a glimpse at mine.

My Big Day!

I was born in the small town of Steinbach, Manitoba, Canada. I lived the first four years of my importance, on a farm. I should not have been around long enough to write this book: Except for the healing power of God, when I was very young. However, God wanted me to be an example for someone to learn from, so that they in turn could be exemplified for another part of humanity, in their saga.

I was also raised in a family where struggles were apart of everyday life. I had women troubles, money troubles, and the same kind of troubles that you had. One of the women troubles that I experienced, was when I was about twelve. I was just a shy young lad, who could hardly look someone else in the face, without turning red as a fireball.

One day, one of the girls in my neighborhood called me on the phone. When they told me that there was a girl on the phone for me, I headed out the door and down the alley: As fast as I could maneuver the obstacles in my way. It was not in the direction of her house. It was in the opposite direction. I was really timid. I am married now, so some things must have changed.

If memory serves me correctly, Jacob had woman problems too. The names and situations were different, but the value for historical, or spiritual values did not differ in the least. God used the incidents concerning the women in my life, to fashion me for purposes useful to Him.

Jacob's exploits are somewhat better known than mine, because he was placed into The Record Book that was to be known throughout time.

Not everybody even knows, or even cares about the Jacob of the Bible. So his short story may never shed any light on some people in history. Nevertheless, some people know me, Jacob Bergen.

Some people have glanced at me to see what I am like. Yet others, have looked and thought, "He is a cheat, a liar, a deceiver."

Another segment of society may have seen me as the kind of person from whom they could learn a positive lesson. Though I have done many rotten things, I have done some right things. All these are set out to learn from. I was a young person once. I had hopes, and dreams. I sang in the church, and I did some speaking when I went out on the evangelistic field with my pastor.

I had hoped to go to Bible school and become a preacher: That did not happen. I had discouragements that caused me sixteen years of wandering from the presence of the LORD.

Jacob Israel had some hopes and dreams when he left home to find a bride. Things did not pan out quite like he had hoped for. He was not exactly walking in the presence of the God of his Fathers. He had his down times.

I have taken the time to contemplate the scenario of my short story. I am going to put it on a hypothetical video for you.

As my life began, I see myself as being like a car headed off in a direction away from God. For some of the time my parents were behind the driver's seat; so the forces of self-destruct did not take all the disastrous turns that I might have taken on my own. At times I jerked the wheel away from them and hit a few trees. However, they would gain control, and pull the car back on the road again. It was a good thing that there was always somebody available to help.

I accepted the LORD as my Savior when I was about twelve. It was then that the wheel of the car was taken over by a better driver, and the highway on which I traveled, was headed to a place of heavenly beauty, where there were no curves in the road.

Then one day the car blew an engine. It was then that I parked it. I said it couldn't be fixed. Although the driver said that it was not a problem that could not be repaired, I insisted that it could not be renewed. I decided to ignore the advice of the LORD, and put it into the parking mode.

I guess I thought that if the motor blew when God was at the wheel, He must have done something wrong, for that to happen. I thought that I would repair it myself and did, at least to the point of running.

In 1965 I cranked up the old jalopy again, (please understand that I am still speaking hypothetically) but I turned it around and headed it for the crevasse: Which was as yet out of my view. I began picking up speed, hit a few trees here and there, I had a few fender benders, and rolled the car. However, that did not stop me.

Although everything was going against me, I kept speeding right along. Sixteen years later, in 1981, I came to a place where I was heading 150 mph., toward the crevasse. I could see it now.

Do you remember the old James Dean movies? The fifties were exciting times. I remember seeing movies where the young guys would play chicken. In some cases it was to impress the girls; while in others instances, it was just to prove to each other who was the bravest.

I can see them now, as they are lined up at a certain distance from the edge of the gorge. The engines are revved up, and I see two teenagers ready to play chicken. The idea is for both of them to come racing toward the edge of the cliff. The first one to put on the brakes is chicken. I was never physically involved in this kind of demonstration on my manhood.

It was a picture of this magnitude that I saw for myself in 1981. There was no stopping me now. However, when I came almost to the very edge of the gorge, there was something within me that said: "You had better put on the brakes right now, or else it will be to late to stop any more."

When I took a trip out to the mountains some years later, I understood how great the danger had been. I worked my way down a steep slope to get myself as close as I could to the edge of a certain cliff. I wanted so badly to see right over the edge, and get a look like the eyes of an eagle would see. I wanted to see what was at the bottom of that gorge.

Suddenly, something within me said, "You had better not get any closer, trust me. If you move in for a closer look, you will be at the bottom of the gorge: And you won't see anything ever again."

I took the advice of the still small voice within me, and I stepped back just a bit. From here, I could be sure that I could continue to appreciate the beauty of all that was at the bottom of that crevasse. It was beauty at its best; there was also danger. I became keenly aware of the danger that can present itself when one gets to close to the edge. Some people like living on the edge. I am not that adventurous.

As I sat on some logs near the edge of this beautiful gorge in the Rocky Mountains, I thought to myself: "If this is the kind of scenario I was in just before the LORD got my attention in 1981, then I was in serious trouble."

If I had not listened to the word of the LORD, which said, "It is time for you Jacob, to stop the car: Now." I felt I would have been at a point of no return.

Until this point in time I had incurred some damages. It was as if I had ripped out the under carriage of the car, when I came screeching to a halt at the edge of the cliff. It was as though I were teetering on the brink of what could have been a bottomless pit. I felt as though I were trapped in the car, pushing all my weight to the back, so that the car would not go over the precipice.

The next move was up to the Master Driver, whom I had ejected from the drivers seat sixteen years earlier. It was He, who was able to distribute the weight to allow me to exit the car, and plant my feet on solid ground again. Once I was safe, the car went over, I saw the wreckage that it caused.

If I were to list some irreparable wreckage caused by me being out of control, I would say that first on the list of importance was: I lost out on the best that God had prepared for me.

Another thing that I could not repair was the broken relationship that I had with my first wife. A child was involved in this marriage. Many other things were lost because of the years I spent speeding around in my old jalopy.

If my life had stopped there, and nothing else had taken place in my life, I could have been thankful that at least my life had been spared. Still, living on from there without having something to replace the losses, would have been tough.

Man is built with the need to have relationships. One of the greatest consolations in the word of God, is found in Joel 2:25&26. Please hear it with me. "I will restore to you the years that the locust hath eaten,…And ye shall eat in plenty, and be satisfied, and praise the name of the LORD your God, that hath dealt wondrously with you: and my people shall never be ashamed."

This is what has happened to me. First, the LORD has restored my relationship with Him. He has given me back a relationship with a woman, the name has changed, but he has once again blessed me with a good wife. We have children, and grandchildren.

I have felt the blessing of the LORD while writing. Maybe the preaching end of ministry that I once sought to be involved in is gone. Nevertheless, He has replaced it with something that I love to do. I love to write.

What lies ahead for me, I don't know, but one thing that I know for sure is: "If God has begun to repair, and rebuild; He will not stop till it is finished." That is something to be thrilled about. One big question I had, that I have found the answer to, is this: "What was it that allowed for the changes that took place, to take place in my life?"

Some people never stopped praying, people like my parents. Joining them was a host of other people called friends. Added to this list were, a few shepherds that prayed for the sheep that had strayed. Hopeless as it may have seemed at times, they kept on the prayer line.

Remember the row of dominoes that I spoke to you of earlier. Well, it was because of prayer, that God could pull out one of the dominoes: So that the rush of dominoes to the edge of the gorge would be halted. If someone had not pulled one of the dominoes, my car would have gone over the precipice, and I would have gone with it.

A little while ago I spoke of the gorge that I visited in the mountains. Another very relevant feature was displayed here. On both sides of the crevasse, there were huge logs that man had arranged. They were the remains of what once was a bridge over the chasm.

Over time something happened to tear down this bridge. I do not know how they even built this bridge over troubled waters, but I know that the water below had taken away whatever support once held the structure. Water is a lifeline, but it also has destructive forces.

What Christ has done in my life, is to become, "The repairer of the breach."

The Lord has asked me, "What is your name?"

He has left me a blank line so I can verify to Him, what that is:

I filled in the line: ***It's Jacob!***

"Now unto the King eternal, immortal, invisible, the only wise God, be Honor and glory forever and ever, Amen." 1Timothy1: 17

We're getting there!

The Final Pages

Ye know not what shall be on the morrow. For what is your life? It is even a vapor that appeareth for a little time, and then vanisheth away. James 4:14

Chapter 19

Life itself is just one great big storybook, comprising of a massive collection of short stories. One may well imagine the amount of color that each of these pictures could generate: If the story were put into picture form. It would be like Jacob's coat of many colors.

The writer of the book of James, articulates it this way:

"...Ye know not what shall be on the morrow. For what is your life? It is even a vapor, that appeareth for a little time, and then vanisheth away." James 4:14

In the light of a statement such as that, each of us is but an expression of a short story. What are 60, 70, 90, or more years, compared with the span of eternity? I know that my life could best be described as a note: In comparison to forever.

I know that I have had some individual experiences that have stayed with me, as though they had enough content to fill the books of eternity for volume. However, in the light of eternity, they too, turned out to be just like a breath of wind. Now you see it, and in a moment it is gone.

Incidents such as these are like millstones about our neck. The apostle Paul describes it as follows:

"...Our light affliction, which is but for a moment." 2Cor.4: 17

I doubt that any of us are any different from another. We differ in appearance, it is a good thing that we do. Nevertheless, in regards to the content of our existence, we could all be classified as: A short story in the Great Book of Life.

In the previous chapter I have shared some of my life's experiences. They comprise a piece or two, to be added to the great jigsaw puzzle of all time. When I look at these in terms of value, I feel as though I would like to place these pieces off behind some bushes, where they cannot be noticed. My life in picture form would look like this, "Oh wretched man, that I am."

Isaiah records another visual, and as I look at it, this is what I see, "Fear not, thou worm, Jacob,...I will help thee."

In myself I am nothing. However, placed where the LORD has me figured in the big picture, I could be of great value. He may take me from out behind the bushes where I have placed my couple of pieces, and He may put them out in the open, but then He may not. His Judgment will count.

Jacob's life begins in Genesis 25, and ends in chapter 49, twenty-five chapters of a continual exegesis of the pieces of his puzzle. We began with a brand-new box of interlocking pieces for Jacob's story.

As we began to assemble them, we were able to enjoy each intricate detail of his span of time, and see the beautiful picture. I am aware that there are many unsightly scenes; many moments portrayed, are of immense beauty. Jacob loved Rachel. This expression of love was exemplified in more than one picture of his life.

Twenty-five Biblical chapters, yet they only came together as a short story. Inter woven into these twenty-five chapters we have the lives of many other people. In great measure they were responsible for how the pieces of Jacob's life came together. By the same token, the reverse is true. Jacob was also accountable for the many pieces that were assembled in the story of Isaac, Rebekah, Laban, Rachel, Leah, Esau, and the list goes on to include his children.

Because of what Jacob was during his pilgrimage, seeing how his deceptive dealings rubbed off on his children is easy. Look at the pictures of Joseph, and also at the time that Jacob's sons deceived Shechem's family.

Each of us has our own short story, but we are not necessarily at center stage in our story. In every case, I believe, that it was others that allowed us to be mirrored into the bright spot from time to time: Then only just to present a reflection for the purposes of highlighting someone else's short story.

Philippians 2:4 says it like this: "Look not every man on his own things, but every man also on the things of others."

It matters not whether your features are that of a woman, or man, boy or girl: At the Judgment seat of Christ, when the LORD asks me, "What's your name?"

I will have to say, "My Name is Jacob."

It is here that I am expecting to hear the most satisfying words I will ever hear, "No, your name is no longer Jacob. Your name is Israel." "Well done, thou good and faithful servant."

When I hear the word servant, I visualize the scene of Jacob's approach to Esau. I can see the change, from him being a grabber (taking all he could for himself), to being a giver. The clip where he bows before Esau and offers to be his servant is a picture of a penitent sinner, in my books.

As one of the segments of my short story, my name was changed to Israel when I received Christ as my personal savior. I picture this as the time when He came to me, and I wrestled with Him, and he blessed me with His love, and eternal life. In a way, my name was changed there.

There is a greater scene that I anticipate viewing someday. That is where I will receive my new name, one that will be written in my forehead. I think that it may be branded in my forehead in big bold letters: "Jacob!"

Cain was branded like this in the early part of the Bible. The mark depicted who he was, as well as telling the world, that he had disobeyed God: As a result he was sent out from the presence of the LORD. However, even in the awful position that Cain found himself in, the grace of God was still extended to him. In some ways it may have been more of an act of mercy, if God had left him to face the world without the mark.

It was because of the mark, that people would keep from killing him. It also left him with the terrible fact of having to live his life in shame. How would you like walking around your place of residence, in your world, branded like that? I for one would not be impressed. It would be as if I were saying, "I am a killer, and a thief. I robbed my brother of a chance of completing his short story."

When we come into the presence of God, we will all come as a marked woman or man: Because our righteousness is as filthy rags. I will never be able to come into His presence, dragging in my personal prizes. All I will ever be able to bring with me is what the Lord has been able to do through me.

Do you remember when the LORD gave out the talents? To one servant He gave ten talents, to another five, and to yet another one talent. All I will be able to do is to say, "LORD, you gave me three talents: I am laying six talents here at Your feet. I did not receive fame and acclaim for it, but I used what you gave me, and I am giving it all to You now."

I will never be able to come before Him and say: "LORD, look what I was able to snatch for myself. I wrangled the blessing from Esau, or I got Rachel. No, a thousand times no.

Someone once said, "Only one life, it will soon be past. Only what is done for Christ will last."

Where do you fit in? Have you come to where you have been changed to start this part of your short story, and allow Jesus Christ access to your life?

Maybe you have already been saved from the penalty of sin, but you have never come to where you were able to bow to God in humble submission: As a servant would do.

Maybe you are still wheeling and dealing in, "The Battle of I'm a Gettin," for Me purposes, instead of for purposes orchestrated to present sweet music to the ears of your Redeemer.

Maybe you have come to a point where in the eyes of God you are complete, and like the apostle Paul speaks of: "You are now ready to be offered, and the time of your departure is at hand."

When you look over the experiences of your short story, I am sure that you have had some regrets. I'm also sure that you must have had some bright spots in your life. When the final pages are written on your life, what will you say when the LORD asks you: What's Your Name?

WHAT'S YOURS?
What's YOURS?
What's YOURS?
What's YOURS?
What's YOURS?
What's YOURS?
What's YOURS?

The End

About the Author

Jacob Bergen is a freelance writer who is in the Floor Covering Business. He has writing in his heart. Jacob has written, edited and published for church magazines. He has written many articles. He has compiled other manuscripts, but this is the first one that has been published. Jacob has a wish to impact people with the written word.

Printed in the United States
4507

9 780759 695351